THE CHICAGO
C·U·B·S

BY DONALD HONIG

Nonfiction

Baseball When the Grass Was Real
Baseball Between the Lines
The Man in the Dugout
The October Heroes
The Image of Their Greatness (*with Lawrence Ritter*)
The 100 Greatest Baseball Players of All Time (*with Lawrence Ritter*)
The Brooklyn Dodgers: An Illustrated Tribute
The New York Yankees: An Illustrated History
Baseball's 10 Greatest Teams
The Los Angeles Dodgers: The First Quarter Century
The National League: An Illustrated History
The American League: An Illustrated History
Baseball America
The New York Mets: The First Quarter Century
The World Series: An Illustrated History
Baseball in the '50s
The All-Star Game: An Illustrated History
Mays, Mantle, Snider: A Celebration
The Greatest First Basemen of All Time
The Greatest Pitchers of All Time
A Donald Honig Reader
Baseball in the '30s
The Power Hitters
1959: The Year That Was
American League MVP's
National League Rookies of the Year
National League MVP's
American League Rookies of the Year
1961: The Year That Was
Baseball: An Illustrated History of America's Game
The Boston Red Sox: An Illustrated History
The St. Louis Cardinals: An Illustrated History

Fiction

Sidewalk Caesar
Walk Like a Man
The Americans
Divide the Night
No Song to Sing
Judgment Night
The Love Thief
The Severith Style
Illusions
I Should Have Sold Petunias
The Last Great Season
Marching Home

THE CHICAGO
C·U·B·S

AN ILLUSTRATED HISTORY

Donald Honig

PRENTICE
HALL
PRESS

New York   London   Toronto   Sydney   Tokyo   Singapore

PRENTICE HALL PRESS
15 Columbus Circle
New York, NY 10023

Library of Congress Cataloging-in-Publication Data
Honig, Donald.
   The Chicago Cubs : an illustrated history / Donald Honig.
     p. cm.
   ISBN 0-13-131327-4 : $24.95
   1. Chicago Cubs (Baseball team)—History. I. Title.
GV875.C6H66 1991
796.357'64'0977311—dc20   90-36300
                                                        CIP

Designed by Robert Bull Design

Manufactured in the United States of America

10 9 8 7 6 5 4 3 2 1

First Edition

For My Daughter, Catherine

Acknowledgments

I am deeply indebted to a number of people for their generous assistance in gathering the photographs reproduced in this book. Special thanks go to Michael P. Aronstein of TV Sports Mailbag; to Patricia Kelly and her colleagues at the National Baseball Hall of Fame and Museum at Cooperstown, New York; and to Steve Gietschier of *The Sporting News*. The remaining photographs are from the following sources: the photograph on the bottom of page 214, Russ Reed; the photograph of Rick Reuschel on page 217, Nancy Hogue; the photograph of Andre Dawson on page 238, Mitchell Layton; the photograph of Mark Grace on page 241, Chuck Rydlewski.

A special thank you also to Bill Deane, chief research assistant at the National Baseball Hall of Fame Library at Cooperstown, and to head librarian Tom Heitz.

For their advice and counsel, a word of thanks to the following: Stanley Honig, Lawrence Ritter, David Markson, Douglas Mulcahy, Mary E. Gallagher, and Louis Kiefer.

And thanks again to my patient and helpful editor, Paul Aron.

CONTENTS

INTRODUCTION

The Chicago Cubs were born with the National League in 1876 and are the only team to have taken the field in every one of the league's seasons, building a record of continuity that is unparalleled in all of baseball.

In the beginning of the twentieth century, at the start of what baseball historians refer to as "the modern era," the Cubs drew a lot of attention by becoming the league's most successful team, winning pennants in 1906, 1907, 1908, and 1910, including an all-time-record major-league win total of 116 in 1906. The team's next era of success came from 1929 to 1938, when the Cubs won four pennants in ten years. The last Cub pennant came in 1945, followed by an interminable dry spell, which attained such proportions that it transformed long-suffering Cub fans from frustrated to philosophical.

One reason Cub fans have been able to tolerate their team's losing ways lies in the familiar, comfortable, and comforting surroundings of Wrigley Field, which is to Cub partisans what Fenway Park is to followers of the Boston Red Sox, a place uniquely their own. Time hallows a place, investing it with memories and creating for each visitor a personal relationship. Nothing can diminish an arena where the great Alexander once pitched; where Hornsby scorched his singular line drives; where Ruth stood and, according to legend, "called his shot"; where late one afternoon in the twilight Hartnett delivered the most resounding home run in the history of Chicago; where Ernie Banks played for nineteen years; where Ryne Sandberg set the standard at second base.

For Chicago Cubs fans, exuberant in their acclaim, fervent in their devotion, admirable in their patience, having their lovable Cubs in Wrigley Field every summer has been delight enough. As one longtime fan put it, "If they won a world championship, sure, we'd be proud. But we couldn't love them any more than we already do."

THE CHICAGO
C·U·B·S

BIRTH OF A TRADITION

LIKE the Red Sox of Boston and the old Dodgers of Brooklyn, the Chicago Cubs have transcended mere reality and become an emotion in the hearts of their followers. A team's supporters must have five qualities for the team to survive; two of them—faith and hope—fans must supply on their own; the other three—loyalty, devotion, and forgiveness—a team must earn. All five have been lovingly and abundantly lavished upon that enduring National League outpost known as the Chicago Cubs.

The National League of Professional Baseball Clubs came into existence in the centennial year of 1876, following the demise of an earlier concoction known as the National Association of Professional Base Ball Players. The National Association, organized in 1871, was the first attempt at a league of professional ball players. With franchises sliding in and out, this jerry-built structure finally collapsed in 1875, thanks to gambling, corrupt players, thrown games, and the public's gradual loss of faith in the game. The Chicago White Stockings were part of the association in 1871, 1874, and 1875.

To some people, the collapse of the National Association signified the end of trying to organize a diverting and enjoyable team sport. Others, however, were not so sure. In its first year of operation, 1871, the circuit's teams had averaged around thirty games each. A year later, the schedule ran closer to fifty games per team; by its last season, 1875, the teams were averaging close to seventy games each. Baseball, evidently, was a lively young

industry, one that possessed the ingredients for success, if it were knowledgeably run and supervised.

One man who had a penetrating vision of baseball's future was William Hulbert, a Chicago businessman, baseball fan, and stockholder in the Chicago White Stockings of the disintegrating National Association. Hulbert not only saw a bright future for the game, he was also aware of the elements that were endangering it. So, late in 1875, he began formulating plans for what would become the National League.

On February 2, 1876, Hulbert was at the Grand Central Hotel in New York City, convening a meeting with like-minded men who were serious about baseball in America and about starting their own league. Sternly and fervently, Hulbert lectured his colleagues about his belief in this game that so entertained and engrossed people, emphasizing how profitable an enterprise it could be if rules and standards for it and for the men who played it were established and strictly enforced.

The founding members of the new league were Chicago, St. Louis, Cincinnati, and Louisville in the west, and New York, Philadelphia, Hartford, and Boston in the east. A seventy-game schedule was drawn up; admission was pegged at fifty cents. Morgan G. Bulkeley, one of Connecticut's more eminent citizens, was chosen league president, though Hulbert was recognized as the organization's strong man. Bulkeley, in fact, served just one year (he soon become governor of Connecti-

2

Morgan Bulkeley, first president of the National League.

cut and later U.S. senator from that state), and Hulbert took over the job, serving until his death in 1882 at the age of forty-nine.

Hulbert provided the strong leadership needed to see the fledgling league through its difficult early years; he was not reluctant to exert his authority. The New York and Philadelphia clubs had decided not to make their final western trips in 1876; sporting woeful won–lost records, their owners saw no point in making swings that would surely result in financial losses. When he took over as president, Hulbert stunned everyone by ousting both franchises from the league, turning the

National League into a six-club operation for the next two years.

As the National League struggled to establish its stability in those early years, franchises dropped in and out with disturbing regularity. Only two of the founding members remained continuously in place year after year—Chicago and Boston. Surviving the rough shoals of the league's early voyages, these two clubs persevered as the National League was joined and abandoned by teams from Buffalo, Indianapolis, Providence, Troy, Syracuse, Worcester, Cleveland, Detroit, Milwaukee, Washington, and Baltimore. This state of affairs lasted until 1900, when the twelve-team league contracted to the eight-team structure that remained intact until 1952: Boston, Brooklyn, Philadelphia, New York, Cincinnati, St. Louis, Pittsburgh, and Chicago. After the 1952 season, the Boston Braves made big-league baseball's first franchise move in half a century when they migrated to Milwaukee. This left the Chicago Cubs with the only uninterrupted history in the National League, a continuity that extends to this day.

So it began in 1876, for the National League and for the Chicago Cubs, who were known then as the White Stockings, in deference to their white hose (long since forgotten as a Cub appellation, the name lives on in connection with Chicago's American League team). It was a time when the pitcher worked from a six-foot-square box, some forty-five feet from the batter, making his delivery in the bowling style of an English cricketer; when it took nine called balls for a batter to walk (after gradual shrinkage, the four-ball rule took effect in 1889); when a batter could request a pitch to be high or low (this was not abolished until 1887).

The 1876 Chicago White Stockings played sixty-six games, won 52, lost 14, and finished in first place, 6 games ahead of runner-up St. Louis. The team employed eleven players all season: eight regulars, two substitutes, and one pitcher.

The pitcher was Albert Spalding, who had

Albert Spalding, when he was starring for the Boston Red Stockings in the early 1870s.

starred with the Boston club in the National Association for five years and who was later to found the sporting goods company that still bears his name. When he set about organizing his new league, Hulbert induced Spalding, who had been born in Illinois, to join Hulbert's Chicago club. Pitching virtually every game, the right-handed Spalding (there were, in fact, no left-handed pitchers in the league as yet) rang up a 47–13 record. He also served as the team's first manager.

Another National Association star that Hulbert talked into coming to Chicago was an infielder/outfielder of the Philadelphia Athletics, Adrian Constantine Anson, soon known as "Cap," who was to become professional baseball's first true superstar and by all accounts the greatest player of the nineteenth century.

Anson was born in Marshalltown, Iowa, on April 11, 1852. He began playing professional

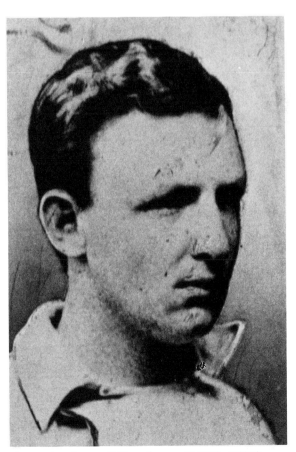

An early photo of Cap Anson (1876–1897).

4

baseball in 1870 and was twenty-four years old when he joined Chicago in 1876. Cap became the team's first baseman in 1879, the same year he took over as manager, holding down his dual jobs until 1897, his last season as an active player.

Anson's achievements were impressive. He was the first man to compile more than 3,000 hits (3,041), had a .334 lifetime average, and guided his team to five first-place finishes. He also won the eternal thanks of Sun Belt innkeepers and winter-weary sportswriters when in March 1882 he introduced the concept of spring training, taking his players to Hot Springs, Arkansas, to sweat out their off-season excesses and get into shape for their summer's work. A tough disciplinarian in a somewhat rowdy and free-wheeling era, Cap insisted on strict observance of his training rules and was not above reinforcing them with his fists, which he was capable of doing if necessary—he was a brawny, 200-pound six-footer, a big man for the time.

Anson, however, was also to inscribe his name on the darker side of baseball's historical ledger. In July 1887 Cap's White Stockings had an exhibition game scheduled against the Newark club of the International League. Newark announced that George Stovey would pitch for them. Stovey was black. (Several dozen blacks had played in the minor leagues and two had appeared with the Toledo club of the American Association, a major league rival of the National League from 1882 to 1891.) When he heard about Stovey, Anson announced he would not allow his team on the field with "a nigger." Newark, instead of telling Anson to go stuff himself, withdrew Stovey from the game, and baseball's unwritten laws of bigotry remained intact until Jackie Robinson crashed through the big-league color barrier in 1947.

As Connie Mack would become with his Philadelphia Athletics and John McGraw with his New York Giants, Anson's identification with his Chicago club became so inseparable in the public mind that, when Cap was finally let go after the 1897 season, the

team was for several years known as "the Orphans."

With pitchers delivering underhand from forty-five feet away, fielders playing without gloves, and teams averaging almost 400 errors each over their seventy-game schedules, statistics from those Dark Age baseball years have little relevance to today's. Nevertheless, Spalding's White Stockings were clearly the class of the league in 1876. The skipper's 47 wins were tops, as were second baseman Ross Barnes's .429 batting average and 138 hits. The team batted .337, seventy points better than third-place Hartford.

The White Stockings played their first two years at a park called the 23d Street Grounds, located not far from the Lake Michigan shore at State Street and 23d, on approximately the same site where the city's National Association club had played.

In 1878 the White Stockings moved to a new home, Lakefront Park, located south of Randolph Street between Michigan Avenue and the Illinois Central tracks. As baseball steadily achieved commercial success, the park was renovated and enlarged in 1883, increasing its capacity to 10,000—largest in the league—including 2,000 grandstand seats and 6,000 in the bleachers, with the remaining ticket holders consigned to standing-room areas. The park even featured a forerunner of today's luxury boxes—eighteen rows of private boxes with curtains and armchairs. Lakefront Park was situated within a few minutes' walk of State Street, the city's chief retail thoroughfare, and was thus convenient for fans who wanted to drop in for a game. For forty-five home dates in 1882, attendance was 130,000, by far the best in the league.

A sore arm made a first baseman of star pitcher Al Spalding in 1877 (Anson was playing third at the time), and without their ace the White Stockings fell to fifth place in what was a six-team league. The club idled to a .500 record in 1878, but a year later began glowing with the stars that would light the way to three straight pennants.

Anson had taken over as manager (and first

George Gore (1879–1886). His .360 batting average in 1880 was tops in the league.

baseman) in 1879 after a one-year stewardship by shortstop Bob Ferguson, whose ability to snap line drives out of the air had earned him the graphic nickname "Death to Flying Things." The White Stockings might have won in 1879 if not for a terrible accident that befell their star pitcher, Terry Larkin. With the team leading the league in early August and Larkin sporting a 31–23 record, a team

Abner Dalrymple (1879–1886), who had a league-high 11 homers in 1885.

6

and personal tragedy occurred. During pre-game practice, the pitcher was struck on the head by a line drive, the impact of which was so great that it not only effectively ended Larkin's career but also deranged him. In 1894 he committed suicide in a Brooklyn mental hospital.

Beginning in 1880, Anson's White Stockings took three straight pennants. These teams included some of the most notable players in early Chicago baseball history. In addition to Anson, the team included infielders Tom Burns and Ned Williamson, outfielders George Gore and Abner Dalrymple, pitchers Larry Corcoran and Fred Goldsmith, and the versatile Mike ("King") Kelly, who played the infield and outfield and also caught.

The popular, talented, high-spirited Mike Kelly (1880–1886).

Next to Anson, Kelly was the most popular man on the team; he was, in fact, one of nineteenth-century baseball's most swash-buckling characters. The King's picture decorated the walls of saloons, barbershops, and poolrooms all over the city. His dashing style, strong good looks, and infectious Irish wit charmed everyone. Mike was a familiar figure in the city's nightlife, in his expensive tailor-made suits, squiring beautiful women, never meeting a bottle he could not empty.

Larry Corcoran, whom Anson said "had the endurance of an Indian pony," was the club's ace pitcher during the glory days of the early 1880s. Starting with a 43–14 record in 1880, Larry was 170–84 during the five full years he pitched for Chicago before a lame arm ended his effectiveness at the age of twenty-five. His triumphs included three no-hitters.

Corcoran's fellow ace, Fred Goldsmith, put in four full years with the White Stockings. Working from 1880 to 1883, he achieved a 98–51 record. According to some baseball historians, it was Goldsmith who delivered the first curveball. On August 16, 1870, the then eighteen-year-old youngster arranged a public demonstration to prove to a largely skeptical audience that, if properly delivered, a ball could indeed be made to curve in midair at the will of the thrower. Setting up three poles in the ground, Goldsmith, working from the then regulation forty-five feet, threw his arcane pitch around the poles over and over again, to the amazed satisfaction of all, including "The Father of Baseball Writers," Henry Chadwick, who reported that "which had ... been considered an optical illusion ... was now an established fact."

Subsequent baseball legend has tended to credit Arthur ("Candy") Cummings with the invention of the curveball. Cummings, who pitched with some success in the National Association and later for two years in the National League, was elected to the Hall of Fame in 1939, chiefly on his claim of having originated the curve. The records show, however, that there was no earlier public demonstra-

Ace pitcher Larry Corcoran (1880–1885).

tion of the innovative pitch than Fred Goldsmith's on August 16, 1870.

Anson's club had a won–lost record of 67–17 in 1880, a winning percentage of .798, enabling them to take the pennant by 15 games over Providence. In 1881, with the skipper batting .399, the White Stockings won by 9 games over Providence, and a year later it was a 3-game victory margin, once again over Providence.

In 1882 William Hulbert died, and Albert Spalding assumed both the ownership and presidency of the White Stockings. The former ace pitcher, already a burgeoning sporting goods tycoon, owned the team until 1902, when he sold out to James Hart.

It remains a curious omission that Hulbert, founder of the National League and through-

out its formative years its sturdy backbone, has never been elected to baseball's Hall of Fame. Morgan Bulkeley, the league's first president, who served for just one year as a distinguished figurehead, was long ago bronzed for Cooperstown, but not Hulbert. Ironically, Hulbert's birthplace, Burlington Flats in upstate New York, lies about ten miles west of Cooperstown. It would be highly appropriate for one of baseball's most significant executives to be "brought home" with honors.

Chicago's reign at the top came to an end in 1883 with a second-place finish, 4 games behind Boston. Joining the team that year was second baseman Fred Pfeffer, whose fielding skills were considered by nineteenth-century baseball enthusiasts to be better than those of Eddie Collins and Nap Lajoie when those icons were setting standards around the bag in the early years of the new century. Pfeffer became part of what was to become known as Chicago's "stonewall infield"—Anson, Pfeffer, Williamson, and Burns—who played together until 1889. Also joining the club that year was outfielder Billy Sunday, who remained with the team until 1887. Never much of a hitter, Billy could run and field. It was not as a ball player, however, that he was destined to leave his mark, but rather as one of the country's most fervent evangelists, singeing the air with his flamboyant oratory until his death in 1935.

Because Lakefront Park had been built to dimensions dictated by certain real-estate constraints, its left-field fence was unusually close to home plate—according to some contemporary accounts, little more than 200 feet away. In the dead-ball era, outfield fences were not built as home-run targets but as park enclosures, and most home runs were legged out inside the park. Nevertheless, even by dead-ball standards, Lakefront Park's left-field wall was considered a bit neighborly, and any ball that took wing over it was a ground-rule double. (Chicago was consistently the league leader in two-base hits, sometimes by wide margins.) Thanks to the wall, Ned William-

8

son led the league in 1883 with the remarkably high total of 49 doubles (in 98 games).

In 1884 the ground rule was changed, thereby transforming those balls hit over the left-field fence from doubles into home runs. Until that time no National Leaguer had ever

hit more than 10 homers in a season, while the record for a team was Boston's 34 in 1883. But with the new ground rule doubling the over-the-fence dividend, in 1884 the White Stockings hit an astounding 142 home runs, which remained the major-league high until broken by the 1927 New York Yankees. Individually, the club had four men with more than twenty homers apiece: Anson 21, Dalrymple 22, Pfeffer 25, and Williamson with a high of 27. Despite this artificially inflated power, the club was never a factor in the pennant race, finishing fourth.

The White Stockings did not have another shot at their inviting left-field wall, for a year later they moved into a new home, West Side Park, located at Congress and Loomis streets. The new arena featured a horseshoe-shaped grandstand with accommodations for 2,500 and a bleacher section with 3,500 seats. For the well-heeled, there were a dozen rooftop boxes furnished with individual chairs. A twelve-foot brick wall enclosed the outfield.

Anson's club prospered in their new surroundings, winning a close-run pennant race with the New York Giants by just 2 games (over a schedule that was now 112 games long). It was the first time that the league's Chicago and New York teams found themselves in hand-to-hand combat for the top spot, creating a rivalry that would peak in intensity two decades later, with distant echoes resounding again in 1969.

Anson's star pitcher was tireless right-hander John Clarkson. The twenty-three-year-old Clarkson had joined the White Stockings late in 1884 and posted a 10–3 record. A year later the Massachusetts-born pitcher scaled the heights with a 53–16 record. When John took a day off, Anson gave the ball to Jim McCormick, who went 20–4.

Tom Burns (1880–1891), posing in a studio ''action'' shot that was typical of the time. The baseball is suspended from the ceiling. Burns was part of Chicago's ''stonewall infield'' in the 1880s.

Billy Sunday (1883–1887), who became one of America's most famous evangelists after his career.

John Clarkson (1884–1887), a prodigious winner in an age of big winners.

In that year a new concept was introduced to baseball, one that would mature in the coming century—a "world series." With the American Association now functioning as a rival major league, it was arranged for both league champions—Chicago in the National League and St. Louis in the American Association—to engage in a postseason seven-game shootout.

This forerunner of what was later to become baseball's premier event was an oddly scheduled business. The first game was played in Chicago, the next three in St. Louis, the fifth in Pittsburgh, and the remaining two in

one year) 24–6. Kelly, playing every position on the field, led the league with a .388 average, while Anson batted .371.

Joining the White Stockings as a regular that year was a twenty-three-year-old outfielder named Jimmy Ryan, who would spend fifteen years with the team and whom many old-time Chicago fans called the greatest outfielder the team ever had. A moody, sometimes sullen man, Ryan was a hustling, crowd-pleasing performer. In his rookie year, he batted .306.

Another postseason series was arranged with the winners in the American Association, again the St. Louis club. With the games divided between the cities of the contending teams this time, St. Louis won four games to the White Stockings' two.

Some people felt that Chicago should have beaten St. Louis, attributing the loss to the rather carefree attitude shown by some of the players. Albert Spalding, whose pride of ownership had been stung by the defeat, shared this feeling. Among the players who had concentrated more on nightlife than day games during the St. Louis series were George Gore, Jim McCormick, and inevitably, King Kelly. Accordingly, that winter Spalding dispatched his three heavy-drinking carousers, dealing Gore to New York, McCormick to Pittsburgh, and the popular Kelly to Boston. Spalding received a then stunning $10,000 for Kelly's contract, a figure so grandiose that the newspapers printed a facsimile of the contract to convince an incredulous public.

Without the King and his jolly cohorts, the White Stockings slipped to third place in 1887, despite Clarkson's 38 wins. The following spring Boston offered Spalding another $10,000, for Clarkson. Spalding took the hefty bait, and the ace pitcher went to Boston, where he joined Kelly in what became known as the "$20,000 battery," the monetary forerunners of Connie Mack's "$100,000 infield" a quarter-century later.

Cincinnati. The series ended inconclusively, with three wins apiece for each team and one game declared a tie.

The schedule was extended to 124 games in 1886, and Anson's club won 90 of them, edging out a strong Detroit team by 2½ games. Clarkson was 35–17, McCormick 31–11, and Jocko Flynn (who pitched only that

John Clarkson, who, like King Kelly, was traded to Boston. There, Clarkson and Kelly became known as the $20,000 battery.

Pitching with modest success for the White Stockings from 1888 to 1889 was a tall right-hander named John Tener, who wound up his brief big-league career with Pittsburgh in 1890. Tener later went into politics and in 1910 was elected governor of Pennsylvania. From 1913 to 1918, he served as president of the National League.

After the 1888 season, during which the White Stockings finished second, Anson took

his club and a team of "All-Americans" on baseball's first world tour. Designed to bring America's game to the shores of the Old World, the teams played in the capitals of Europe and went as far as Cairo, where a game was played in the shadows of the pyramids. A contemporary newspaper carried the following account:

> The Spalding party drew up in front of the Hotel d'Orient, the Chicagos mounted on donkeys, the Americans on camels and the ladies in carriages and in this order started through the town led by Anson. The cavalcade proceeded directly over the Bridge Kasielnil and along the Nile to the village of Ghizeh, through a double line of shouting and wondering natives, who were quite unable to make the affair out.

After forty centuries, the stolid sphinx probably thought it had seen everything. Not quite.

Dissatisfied with what they deemed the owners' unfair treatment (low salaries, salary limits, arbitrary fines and suspensions, and other complaints), the players in 1886 formed their first union, the Brotherhood of Ballplayers. The Brotherhood's principal aims were to eliminate the reserve clause (a contractual lasso that bound a man to a team until the team decided upon some modification of the arrangement) and do away with salary limitations, which were then $2,000 a year.

The owners never took the Brotherhood seriously, and the players' requests were generally ignored. The players decided the only solution would be to form their own league. Thus, in 1890 the Players' League was born; with the American Association still functioning, this gave the country three major leagues playing simultaneously. It proved to be too many.

The Players' League lasted but one year, and when it departed it took with it the American Association, which had suffered deep and irrecoverable financial losses during the three-league season. From 1892 until the arrival of the American League in 1901, the

Bill Hutchinson (1889–1895), who led the National League in victories in 1890, 1891, and 1892.

Bill Dahlen (1891–1898), one of the fine shortstops of Chicago's early years.

National League had a monopoly on baseball in America.

The brief adventures of the Players' League also took a toll on the Chicago White Stockings. With the exception of Anson, third baseman Tom Burns, and pitcher Bill Hutchinson, the entire team bolted to help form the new league. With little time to spare, Anson had to rebuild his team, doing it so quickly and effectively that the club (which finished second) captured the imagination of local fans, who began calling the youngsters "the Colts."

The 1890s passed uneventfully for the Chicago team, with 1891's second-place finish their best of the decade. With the demise of the American Association, the National League became a twelve-team circuit, an unwieldy structure that lasted until 1900.

The decade, in retrospect, allowed major-league baseball to fine-tune itself in preparation for the twentieth century and a future of spectacular growth, development, and expansion. Much significant tinkering took place in this decade. In 1893 the pitching distance was increased from fifty feet to sixty feet six inches (those extra six inches are due to an early mismeasurement that was never corrected), and the pitcher was required to work from a rubber slab. In 1894 a bunted foul was declared a strike. In 1895 the infield fly rule was adopted, and that same year it was stipulated that bats could not exceed forty-two inches in length nor two and one-half inches in diameter. In 1899 the balk rule was established, requiring a pitcher to throw to first base if a move was made in that direction.

Some excellent players performed for the Chicago "Colts" during the closing decade of the century, including shortstop Bill Dahlen (he had a 42-game hitting streak in 1894), first baseman/third baseman Bill Everett, outfielder Bill Lange, and pitchers Nixey Callahan and Clark Griffith.

Frank Chance, a budding Chicago hero who joined the team in 1898, called Lange unequaled as a center fielder. A brawny, handsome six-footer, Lange played from 1893 through 1899, when at the age of twenty-eight he retired to marry the daughter of a wealthy San Francisco real estate magnate. Bill, who peaked at .389 in 1895, left behind a .330 lifetime average.

Griffith, a crafty right-hander, pitched for Anson's club from 1893 through 1900, when he jumped to the Chicago White Sox (whom he also managed) of the newly formed American League. The future and longtime owner of the Washington Senators, he was a twenty-game winner six years in a row.

Malachi Kittredge, who caught for Chicago from 1890–1897.

Frank Chance (1898–1912) as a rookie in 1898.

In 1893 the team moved to a new home, West Side Grounds, where they remained until taking over Wrigley Field in 1916. This field, where the Chicago Cubs were to enjoy the greatest success in their history, was located at Polk and Lincoln (now Wolcott) streets. On April 30, Chicago's first double-deck ballpark set what was then an all-time one-game attendance record when 27,489 fans came out to watch their heroes blank St. Louis, 4–0.

In 1897 the forty-six-year-old Anson announced that this would be his final year as an active player. On July 18, the skipper collected his 3,000th hit, the first man in baseball history to attain what was to become a benchmark achievement for future big-league hitters.

The following February, much to the dis-

Clark Griffith (1893–1900), at the beginning of his lifelong career in baseball.

Cap Anson, who had a lifetime batting average of .334 in his twenty-two-year career with Chicago.

may of his idolizing fans, Anson was dismissed as manager. Cap had long been bickering with club president James Hart, but as long as Anson starred at first base, Hart had been reluctant to lose his services. But whereas Anson the player had not been expendable, Anson the manager immediately was. With Spalding's concurrence, Chicago's first baseball institution was let go.

Anson took over as manager of the New York Giants in 1898 but lasted for just twenty-two games, quit, and never returned to baseball. Anson, who died in Chicago on April 14, 1922, three days before his seventieth birthday, spent his postbaseball years running a billiard parlor, appearing on vaudeville stages (many famous athletes did a turn on the stage in those years), and serving as Chicago's city clerk.

For those who had seen him play from 1876 to 1897, Anson was the automatic choice as the game's all-time first baseman. Not until the arrival of the sleek-fielding George Sisler and his .400 bat in the 1920s and then the lethal slugging of Lou Gehrig soon thereafter, was Cap finally toppled from his pedestal.

HEADING FOR GREATNESS

T HE Chicago Cubs—as they were to become known with the turning of the century—had long been dominated by their manager–first baseman Cap Anson. Echoing that tradition, the year after Anson's departure marked the arrival of another man who, as first baseman and manager, would lead the team through its era of greatest success—Frank Chance.

Chance, whose powerful physique and bruising fists earned him the nickname "Husk," was born in Fresno, California, on September 9, 1877. Originally aspiring to a career in dentistry, he enrolled at Washington College in Irvington. In a later era, he probably would have received an athletic scholarship, but in Chance's time colleges were guided by educational standards and not diverted by athletic profits. To help pay his way through cavities and root canals, the young man began playing semipro ball in the area. In 1898, recommended by fellow Californian Bill Lange, Chance was invited by the Chicago club to their spring-training camp in West Baden Springs, Indiana, where he made enough of an impression to be offered a contract.

The man who was to become one of the most celebrated of all first basemen broke into the big leagues as a catcher, backing up the regular backstop, Tim Donahue. The team liked the youngster's abilities, his intelli-

The Cubs' longtime first baseman, Frank Chance.

Tom Burns, who ended his playing career for Chicago in 1891, managed the club in 1898–1899.

gence, his ruggedness. One contemporary writer said of Chance, "When he was given the opportunity to work behind the bat, he stopped the pitched balls with the ends of his fingers, the foul tips with his knees, and the wild pitches with the top of his head." But the young man, the writer noted, "could take the punishment and come back for more." These accolades were particularly noteworthy in an era when baseball was a much harder game, when tolerance for pain was part of a man's résumé; for a rookie—they were not especially welcome in those days of seventeen-man rosters—to make so marked an impression with his grit was unusual.

Tom Burns, the team's former third baseman, managed from 1898 to 1899; from 1900 to 1901 the skipper was Tom Loftus. Neither man had much success.

In 1901 Ban Johnson, president of the Western League, long the strongest of the minor leagues, upgraded his circuit to major-league status, by eliminating the despised reserve clause and raiding National League talent with lures of higher salaries. The new American League opened with teams in eight cities, including Chicago. The new team, owned by Charles Comiskey, appropriated the old familiar Chicago name of White Stockings, which the newspapers soon shortened to White Sox.

With the new league offering enticing contracts backed by fresh new money and the old league behaving like any self-respecting mo-

Outfielder Sam Mertes (1898–1900). Like many other Chicago players, Mertes bolted for the riches of the new American League.

Rube Waddell (1901). Nothing seemed screwed on very tightly, except for that left arm.

whose departing opportunity seekers included first baseman John Ganzel, third baseman Bill Bradley, outfielder Sam Mertes, and star pitchers Clark Griffith and Nixey Callahan. The following year they lost outfielder Topsy Hartsel and pitchers Tom Hughes and Rube Waddell.

It is barely remembered today that the eccentric, spectacularly talented Waddell pitched for the Cubs, but indeed he did, in 1901, posting a 13–15 record before jumping to the Philadelphia Athletics of the newly hatched American League, where he became a big winner, a six-time strikeout leader, and one of baseball's all-time cuckoo clocks (he would disappear for days at a time during the season to go fishing, he loved to hang around firehouses and to chase after the engines, he was married more times and missed more alimony payments than he or the law could remember; he did everything to excess, including drinking whiskey and eating ice cream, and when he died at the age of thirty-seven in 1914 his fastball was gone but his innocence was still intact).

Along with the rubber-headed Waddell, the Cubs also had at the time one of baseball's great rubber-armed pitchers, Jack Taylor. This durable right-hander was with the team from 1898 to 1903, when he was traded to the St. Louis Cardinals, and then again from 1906 to 1907. During one stretch, from June 20, 1901, to August 9, 1906, Taylor started and completed 187 consecutive games, the major-league record. Even in an era when pitching a complete game was the norm, this feat was impressive.

The Cubs had a new manager in 1902, Frank Selee, former longtime skipper of the Boston Braves, with whom he had won five pennants in the 1890s. Selee won no pennants in Chicago, but it was his experienced guidance that put together the team that be-

nopoly (the National League had imposed a $2,400 salary cap), National League players began packing their suitcases and heading for American League ports. Among the clubs hardest hit by these defections were the Cubs,

20

Frank Selee, who built the machine that Frank Chance ran so brilliantly.

The lead man on what would become baseball's most famous double-play combination, Joe Tinker, took over at shortstop in 1902, beginning an eleven-year tenure, during which his fielding was ranked second only to that of Honus Wagner (any shortstop who was a contemporary of Wagner's could aspire only to second-best in any category). Although he was a .263 lifetime hitter, Tinker had the uncanny knack of rapping clutch hits against the league's greatest pitcher, New York's Christy Mathewson.

Joining the club that September was second baseman Johnny Evers. The five-foot nine-inch Evers, who never weighed more than 125 pounds, played second base for the Cubs until 1913. He was tough, aggressive, brainy, and often testy (one of his nicknames was "the Crab," a testament as much to his sometimes grainy disposition as to the way he sidled up to ground balls). A lifetime .270 hitter, his alert baseball mind was responsible for the game's most famous on-the-field episode

came the powerhouse victory machine of the early twentieth century. So many new young players were introduced at the West Side Grounds at this time that the team was nicknamed "the Cubs." The team had been called the Orphans after Anson's departure, then the Remnants after the American League defections, and then the Colts. All these were, of course, informal labels, as was Cubs, but it was the latter that finally stuck.

A look at the 1902 club, which finished fifth, shows solid contours beginning to take shape. Frank Chance was now starting to appear at first base, a position he at first disdained. He had been hoping to become the regular catcher, but that spot had been brilliantly filled by Johnny Kling, who came to be regarded by many as the league's top catcher throughout the century's first decade.

Catcher Johnny Kling (1900–1908, 1910–1911).

Joe Tinker (1902–1912, 1916).

of chaos—the celebrated "Merkle's Boner" controversy of 1908—that led to a Chicago pennant. On September 15, 1902, the first Tinker-to-Evers-to-Chance double play was executed at West Side Grounds, and a bit of imperishable baseball lore was born. The combination eventually inspired a piece of oft-quoted doggeral whose longevity has been the envy of many a fine poet. In 1910 New York journalist and Giant fan Franklin P. Adams, having had another afternoon at the ballpark clouded by the Cubs' snappy DP unit, returned to his office and wrote the following:

These are the saddest of possible words—
Tinker to Evers to Chance
Trio of bear cubs and fleeter than birds,
Tinker to Evers to Chance

Thoughtlessly pricking our gonfallon
  bubble,
Making a Giant hit into a double,
Words that are weighty with nothing but
  trouble—
Tinker to Evers to Chance.

It was entitled "Baseball's Sad Lexicon," and it has taken its place at the apex of baseball's pyramid of literature, along with "Take Me Out to the Ball Game" and "Casey at the Bat."

Some spoilsport researchers have since uncovered the fact that, numerically at least, the Cub trio was not the most efficient of double-play makers (though let us assume they performed their ruinous ritual with flash and élan). Adams's poem has been cited as responsible for the three being elected to the

21

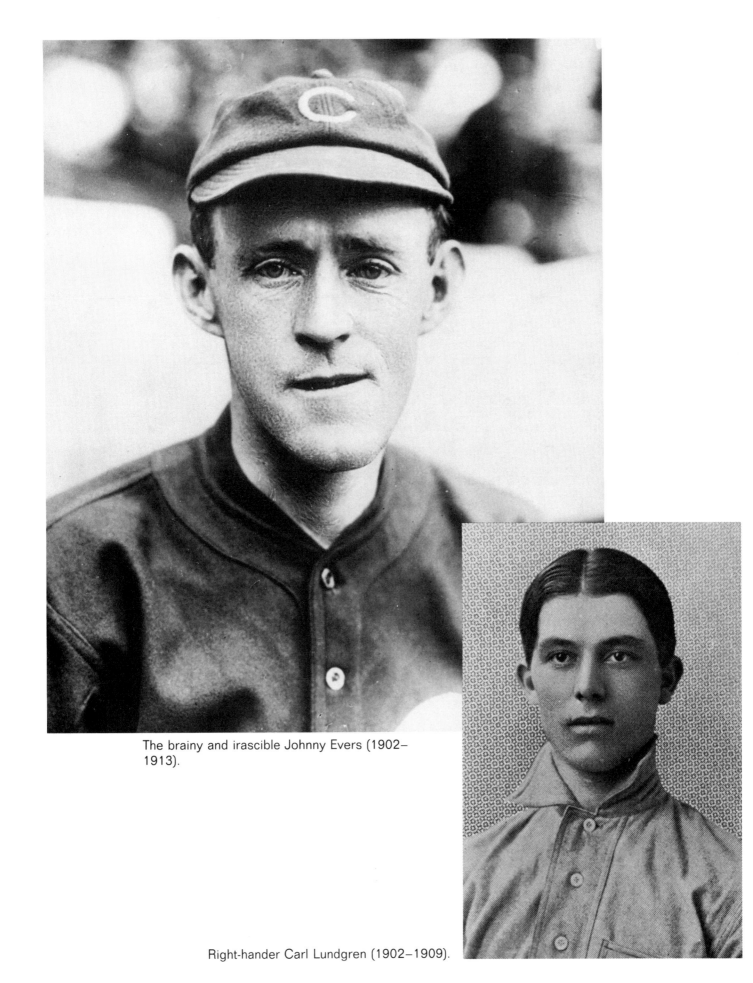

The brainy and irascible Johnny Evers (1902–1913).

Right-hander Carl Lundgren (1902–1909).

Hall of Fame as a unit in 1946, and thus they have remained. (Reality, as ever, is less romantic: Tinker and Evers detested one another and for years after a 1905 fistfight would not speak to each other off the field.)

Also part of the coming cast of stars in 1902 were outfielder Jimmy Slagle, who possessed strong defensive skills (history fails to tell us why, but one of his nicknames was "the Human Mosquito"), and right-hander Carl Lundgren, a winning pitcher who would be overshadowed on the great Cub staff that was developing.

In 1903 Selee's rebuilding began to show positive results as the team ran up a respectable 82–56 record, with a third-place finish. Jack Taylor was 21–14, thirty-year-old rookie Jake Weimer was 21–9, and Bob Wicker, 19–10.

A bit of suspected chicanery that year led to the Cubs making one of the landmark transactions in their history. Starting in 1903, and for many years thereafter, the Cubs and White Sox engaged in a postseason City Series for bragging rights to the sidewalks of Chicago. In the 1903 competition—it ran for fourteen games, with each side winning seven—some of Jack Taylor's losing performances carried an unpleasant aroma. Although never proven, there were rumors that Jack's ethics and shoddy pitching were of equal quality, inspired by tainted money. Consequently, the Cubs decided to unload him, and on December 12, 1903, he was sent to the Cardinals as part of a deal that brought to the Cubs the man who was about to become the greatest of all their pitchers—Mordecai Peter Centennial ("Three-Finger") Brown.

Brown's famous nickname derived from a childhood accident in which his right hand lost an argument with a corn shredder. By the time the boy had snatched his hand back from the machine, he had lost most of his index finger and suffered serious injuries to his pinky and middle finger. This was most painful to little Mordecai and most distressing to his family, but it was destiny's way of having sec-

Lefty Jake Weimer (1903–1905), who won 59 games in his three seasons with Chicago.

ond thoughts about the youngster's future, for the reshaped configuration on his hand enabled Brown to throw a curveball with an exceedingly sharp downward break, forcing batters to hit the ground balls that were to make Tinker, Evers, and Chance famous.

Brown came to the big leagues with the Cardinals in 1903 and showed some promise with a 9–13 rookie year. The St. Louis management, however, felt that his battered right hand would be a handicap and prevent Brown from becoming a star, a decision that would prove to be completely wrong-headed.

Selee's 1904 Cubs were 93–60 during the first year of the 154-game schedule, finishing

Mordecai Peter Centennial Brown (1904–1912, 1916), better known
as ''Three-Finger.'' Note the stub of forefinger on his right hand.

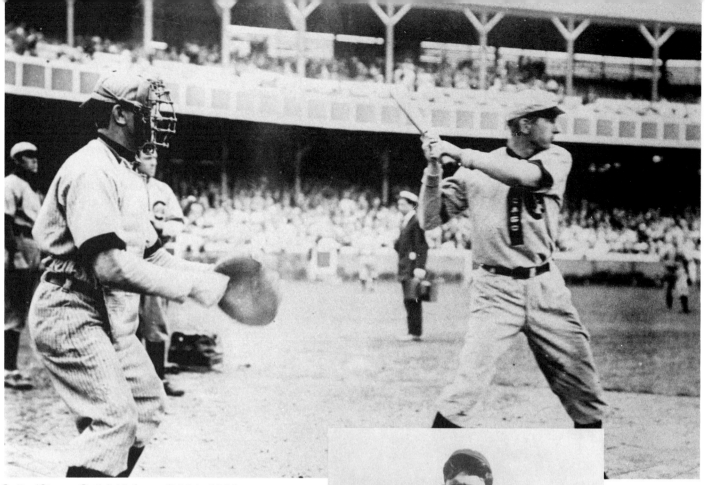

Solly (Circus Solly) Hofman (1904–1911, 1916) taking batting practice at New York's Polo Grounds. Note that catchers were not yet wearing shin guards.

second to a powerful John McGraw team that took the pennant by 13 games. Weimer was a 20-game winner again (20–14), Buttons Briggs was 19–11, Lundgren 17–10, Wicker 17–8, and Brown 15–10. Outfielders Frank ("Wildfire") Schulte and Solly Hofman, who would play important roles in the team's future success, also joined the Cubs that year. Though an outfielder by trade, Hofman possessed a versatility that made him invaluable; during his career he played every position except pitcher and catcher.

The 1905 club also posted a strong winning record of 92–61, which earned them third place. Wicker and Briggs had begun to

Outfielder Billy Maloney, who played just one year for the Cubs (1905) and led the league with 59 stolen bases.

decline, but Weimer, Brown, and newcomer Ed Reulbach were 18-game winners. Weimer, who won 59 games in his three Chicago seasons, was traded in March 1906 to Cincinnati for third baseman Harry Steinfeldt, who for

years was the answer to a favorite trivia question: who played third base on the Tinker, Evers, Chance infield? Steinfeldt had talents other than his sure glove, strong arm, and solid bat. Stagestruck as a boy, he had been part of a touring minstrel show when he decided to try his hand at professional baseball.

Selee had done an excellent job rebuilding the team, but the skipper would not be able to reap the harvest for which he had so diligently worked. Wracked by the tuberculosis that would take his life four years later, he had begun making fewer road trips with the team. When the manager was indisposed, he handed the reins of authority to first baseman Frank Chance, whose leadership qualities had long been apparent. Finally, on August 1, the ailing Selee was forced to resign.

Club owner Charles W. Murphy, who had recently bought out the interests of James Hart, appointed Chance as manager. It was the beginning of one of the finest managerial tenures in baseball history—from 1906 through 1910, the Cubs would post 530 victories, an average of 106 per year, a record no other team has ever approached.

If anyone ever asks who played third base for the Cubs before Harry Steinfeldt, tell them it was James (Doc) Casey (1903–1905).

T·H·R·E·E

THE GREATEST YEARS

CHARLES Murphy was anxious to have a winner, and in 1906 his employees gave him the most relentless and sumptuous of winners, a team so excellent that never in baseball history had there been one like it, nor has there since.

Frank Chance's team went to a decision 152 times that season and on 116 of those occasions came away a winner, posting a 116–36 record and a .763 winning percentage. The nearest any club has come to this prodigious record is the 111 victories compiled by the 1954 Cleveland Indians.

Illustrating Chicago's high-caliber dominance in 1906 is the fact that the second-place New York Giants won 96 games and were never really in the race, finishing 20 games behind the Cubs, who were 80 games over .500. Pittsburgh was 93–60, setting a record for a third-place team with .608 percentage. Among many achievements that year, the Cubs set an all-time major-league standard by winning 60 games on the road, ending with a remarkable road record of 60–15. Included in this triumphant summer was a 26–3 August, a club mark for one-month success.

The Cubs set a club record with 283 stolen bases, made the fewest errors (194), had the highest fielding average (.969), the lowest earned run average (1.76), and the highest batting average (.262).

Steinfeldt (.327), Chance (.319), and Kling (.312) were the team's top hitters, with Steinfeldt's 176 hits and 83 RBIs leading the league. Chance's 57 stolen bases also led the

Harry Steinfeldt (1906–1910), the other member of Chicago's famous infield.

league (in 1903 he had set a still-standing team record with 67 thefts). Schulte led the club with 7 homers and the league with 13 triples.

The pride of Chicago that year was the Cub pitching staff, as stingy a group of men as ever worked a big-league mound—their collective ERA of 1.76 was largely the work of six men.

Frank Chance.

Their individual records and earned run averages read like this:

Three-Finger Brown	26–6	1.04
Jack Pfiester	20–8	1.56
Ed Reulbach	19–4	1.65
Carl Lundgren	17–6	2.21
Jack Taylor	12–3	1.83
Orval Overall	12–3	1.88

Pfiester, a left-hander, had become a regular starter that year; Overall, a big right-hander, had been obtained in a June trade with Cincinnati, and ex-Cub Taylor had been reacquired from St. Louis in July. Brown was the ace of aces, spinning 10 shutouts.

While it is true that earned run averages were uniformly lower in the dead-ball era, the Cub staff in those years was remarkably effi-

Frank Schulte (1904–1916).

cient. No pitching staff in National League history has ever compiled a composite ERA of under 2.00, with the prominent exception of Frank Chance's men, who did it three times, in 1906, 1907, and 1909.

Another new member of the team was outfielder Jimmy Sheckard, a good all-around player. Already a nine-year veteran at the age of twenty-seven, Jimmy came to the Cubs in a trade with Brooklyn, with whom he had put in some excellent years.

In 1906 sixteen big-league teams were fielded, representing eleven different cities. There were two teams apiece in Boston, Chicago, Philadelphia, and St. Louis, and three in New York. Boston and Philadelphia never had an all-city World Series, St. Louis had just one (in 1944), while New York, of course,

Three-Finger Brown. His lifetime ERA of 2.06 is third best in baseball history.

Jack Pfiester (1906–1911), who was a 20-game winner in 1906 and had a league-best ERA of 1.15 in 1907.

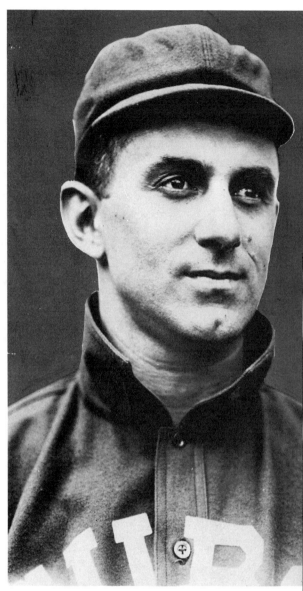

Ed Reulbach (1905–1913), one of the most difficult pitchers in baseball history to defeat.

Right-hander Orval Overall (1906–1913), who had a stellar ERA of 1.58 in four World Series for Chicago.

had many. Only once has the city of Chicago been host to a crosstown World Series—in 1906.

If ever a World Series mismatch seemed to be looming, it was the 1906 affair. The White Sox, who rode to the pennant on the unlikely wings of a 19-game September winning streak, have been remembered in baseball history as "the Hitless Wonders." They batted a collective .230, lowest in the American League. They did, however, have some first-class pitching in right-handers Frank Owen and Ed Walsh and lefties Nick Altrock and Doc White. Nevertheless, it was widely assumed that the Cubs, such prodigious winners all year and clearly the stronger team, would win easily.

The World Series, however, is a pageant designed for surprises, from both teams and individuals. The 1954 Cleveland Indians, for example, were winners of an American League–record 111 games; they went into their World Series against the New York Giants and were swept in four straight.

The 1906 Series lasted for six games, which in itself surprised a lot of people who thought the Cubs would win in four; the bigger surprise, though, was that the White Sox emerged as world champions.

The White Sox won the opener, 2–1, Altrock beating Three-Finger Brown, the game played on a piercing cold day that included snow flurries. The Cubs evened things the next day when Reulbach pitched a 7–1, 1-hit victory. (Another Cub pitcher, Claude Passeau, would equal Reulbach's sparkler with a one-hitter against Detroit in the 1945 World Series. These games remained the low-hit standards in World Series competition until the Yankees' Don Larsen pitched nine perfect innings against the Dodgers in 1956.)

Ed Walsh came near to duplicating Reulbach's effort the next day, when he gave up just 2 hits in shutting down the Cubs, 3–0, beating Pfiester. It remained a pitchers' Series in Game 4, when Brown delivered a 2-hitter of his own, nipping Altrock and the Sox, 1–0.

Jimmy Sheckard (1906–1912), Chicago's multi-talented outfielder.

After Game 4, the White Sox suddenly, unexpectedly, and astonishingly cranked up their hitting, winning Game 5, 8–6 on 12 hits, and then becoming world champions with a 14-hit, 8–3 Game 6 win. After collecting just 11 hits in the first four games, the hitting the White Sox did in the final two games seemed positively thunderous.

"They simply came out and beat us," Chance said later. "That is the nature of

Three-Finger Brown displaying some razzle-dazzle for the photographer.

baseball. It was fair and square." That was his statement for the record. What the skipper said privately to Three-Finger Brown was different. "After the last game," Brown told pitcher Burleigh Grimes years later, "Chance came over to me in the clubhouse and said, 'How that goddamn ball club ever beat us, I'll never understand.' "

The 1907 Cubs were almost as hard to beat as the 1906 record setters, rampaging to a 107–45 record and another runaway pennant, finishing 17 games ahead of second-spot Pittsburgh. Again stingy pitching—this time the stingiest in history—spearheaded the team's success. Once more the roll call of Cub pitchers and their reigning statistics is all-telling:

Orval Overall	23–8	1.70
Three-Finger Brown	20–6	1.39
Carl Lundgren	18–7	1.17
Jack Pfiester	15–9	1.15
Ed Reulbach	17–4	1.69

This staff was responsible for a 1.73 ERA, the lowest in baseball history. Granted, this was during an era of modest run production, when a home run was something of a freak occurrence, when teams averaged less than four runs a game. The fact is, however, that only seven National League pitchers in 1907 logged ERAs under 2.00, and five of them worked for the Cubs. The staff's efficiency was no doubt abetted by the league's sharpest defense—for the third year in a row, the Cubs led in fewest errors and highest fielding average.

In winning 107 games, the Cubs were without a single .300 hitter, Chance's .293 topping the regulars. The team hit just 13 home runs, one above the all-time low for a Cub team, set in 1905.

Chicago's opponents in the 1907 World Series were the Detroit Tigers, who were led by the most intense and successful hitter ever to play America's game, twenty-year-old Tyrus Raymond Cobb. The slim, mercurial young Georgian had won the first of his nine successive (of twelve total) batting titles with

A rare action photo from the 1906 World Series. It is the top of the sixth inning of Game 3, the White Sox have the bases loaded, and Jack Pfiester is trying to work out of the jam. He fanned the batter he is facing here (Frank Isbell), but the next man cleared the bases with a triple, giving the White Sox a 3–0 victory. Notice how shallow the outfielders played in the dead-ball era.

a .350 average. Along with Cobb and the hard-hitting Sam Crawford, some also believed Detroit had the pitching to match Chicago's in 25-game winners Wild Bill Donovan and Ed Killian, plus George Mullin and Ed Siever.

In the opener in Chicago, the Cubs received a big break. Trailing 3–2 with two out in the bottom of the ninth and the tying run on third, pinch-hitter Del Howard struck out, only to see the ball get away from catcher Charlie Schmidt, allowing the tying run to score. Thus reprieved, the Cubs went on to play a 3–3 tie, the game being called after the twelfth inning because of darkness. Overall pitched the first nine; Reulbach, the final three. Chicago's game was highlighted by a single-game Series-record 7 stolen bases.

After that, Chicago pitching bore down with the full weight of those parsimonious

The famous double-play combination. *Left to right:* Joe Tinker, Johnny Evers, Frank Chance.

earned run averages. Pfiester won, 3–1; Reulbach won, 5–1; Overall won, 6–1; and then Brown put it to sleep with a 2–0 victory in the finale. The Cub staff allowed just 4 earned runs in 48 innings, posting a scintillating 0.75 ERA. Most notably, they held Cobb to just 4 hits in 20-at bats. Steinfeldt was the hitting star for the Cubs, with 8 hits and a .471 average.

The Cubs warming up before a game at West Side Park in 1908.

That's Johnny Evers taking a leap and a bound as he tries to score, but New York Giants catcher Roger Bresnahan seems to be waiting for him. In 1915 Bresnahan would become manager of the Cubs.

The relentless onslaught of Chicago pitching quickly disheartened the Detroit fans; coupled with some cold blustery weather when the Series moved to Detroit, attendance declined in the final two games to 11,306 and than a meager 7,370.

For glory, drama, and excitement in their purest forms, the 1908 season stands apart in Chicago Cub history. Chance's boys won a third straight pennant, but unlike the previous two, which were like processional marches through the league, this one left nails bitten to the quick. This was one of those pennant races by which baseball measures its cycle through the universe. It wasn't just a close race, it was a close race between the Cubs and the New York Giants, and if there was one thing more savory to a Cub fan than winning a pennant, it was snatching the banner from John McGraw's Giants.

The Cubs held first place until mid-July, then relinquished it to the Pirates, with the Giants staying close. In early August the Pirates were in first place, the Giants second, and the Cubs third, 4 games out. In mid-September it was still close, with just 2 games separating the three top teams. On September 22 the Cubs swept a doubleheader at the

The quick-thinking Johnny Evers, who retrieved the ball and forced Fred Merkle at second base in the infamous "Merkle's Boner" game on September 23, 1908.

Polo Grounds to move within ½ game of the first-place Giants. This set the stage for the September 23 game, destined to become the most controversial in baseball history.

The game went into the bottom of the ninth inning in a 1–1 tie, with Pfiester and Christy Mathewson dueling. With one out Giant Art Devlin singled. Devlin was forced at second on Moose McCormick's grounder. Fred Merkle, the Giants' young first baseman, then singled, sending McCormick to third with the potential winning run. (Because of the illness of regular first baseman Fred Tenney, the nineteen-year-old Merkle was starting his first game of the year.) The next batter, Al Bridwell, drew cheers and cries of exultation with a base hit into center field,

scoring McCormick with the winning run. Or what seemed to be the winning run.

Baseball rules dictated that a runner in Merkle's situation must touch second base in order for the run to count; otherwise he was leaving himself vulnerable to a force out, which would nullify the run. Baseball tradition at that time, however, held that the game was over the moment the winning run scored, and the rule was not enforced.

There was, however, a preamble to the chaos that was about to erupt at the Polo Grounds. The same situation had occurred in Pittsburgh in a game between the Cubs and Pirates on September 4: with the bases loaded in a scoreless tie in the bottom of the tenth, a Pirate one-bagger had scored a run. The Pirate runner on first observed custom and never touched second, as the rules demanded. This oversight was spotted by Johnny Evers, who got the ball and stepped on second. But the umpire, Hank O'Day, was leaving the field and was therefore unable to certify whether the Pirate base runner had touched second base or not. The Cubs protested the game, but the protest was disallowed.

Now the same situation was happening again, and interestingly enough the umpire involved was once again Hank O'Day (who had never disputed the legitimacy of Evers's claim but simply stated that the baserunning omission had gone unobserved).

When Evers realized that Merkle had not touched second and was not going to, Johnny called for the ball. This time O'Day was alert to what was happening. At this point the whole affair becomes mired in confusion, amid a welter of conflicting stories. Seeing the Cubs' plan, some of the Giants tried to get Merkle back and have him touch the bag. A ball came in from the outfield, heading for Evers. It was intercepted by Giant Joe McGinnity who, some say, threw it into the crowd, which was now pouring onto the field, whooping it up on the green grass where the Giants had just—they believed—won a crucial victory.

Then another ball appeared, from where

and with what authenticity, no one knows. However the force out of Fred Merkle began, it was successfully completed when Johnny Evers, ball in hand, stepped on the bag before Merkle could get to it.

With the force out, the inning was over. The game was still tied. But a large part of the estimated twenty-thousand customers were now on the field, and some of them were beginning to realize what had happened and were involving themselves in it. There was some wrestling about with Cub players, some punches were thrown, and when the umpires saw it would be futile to try to continue, they called it a day.

Two days later, National League president Harry Pulliam supported O'Day and declared that the disputed game was a 1–1 tie. Cub owner Charles Murphy had tried to convince Pulliam to give his club a 9–0 forfeit victory because the Giants, as the home team, were responsible for clearing the field, but Pulliam refused to give the Cubs the game on what one newspaper called "a cowardly technicality."

Originally there were no plans to reschedule the game, but at the end of the season, it became necessary when the Cubs and Giants finished with identical 98–55 records, ½ game ahead of the Pirates, who were 98–56. It was the first time that two clubs had ended the season deadlocked. The now-famous tie game of September 23 would have to be played to a decision. This was not a playoff but a make-up game (the first pennant playoff between teams tied for first place at the end of the season did not occur until Brooklyn and St. Louis had to settle the 1946 pennant).

The National League's momentous deciding game was scheduled for October 8 at the Polo Grounds.

Giant fans were naturally hostile to the Cubs, and after the "Merkle incident," the Polo Grounds reception for the Cubs was angry, profane, and threatening. A cordon of police was assigned to guard the Chicago dugout during the game.

Unquestionably, the person praying hard-

Hank O'Day, the umpire who made the courageous call at the Polo Grounds. O'Day would later manage the Cubs.

est for a Giant victory was young Fred Merkle (sitting on the bench for this one), who had been brutally criticized and ridiculed by the New York press for his failure to touch second base. One man who staunchly defended the youngster was John McGraw, who realized that what Merkle had done—or not done—was common practice. One writer said, with a touch of irony and prescience, "Merkle's best chance to go down in baseball history is for the Giants to lose today. At least a dozen persons will then remember him for life." The writer certainly knew what would attract posterity's attention, but he was wrong in estimating how far and wide the name of Merkle would resound.

With Brown having worked in eleven of the Cubs' previous fourteen games, Chance started Pfiester, while the Giants, inevitably, countered with Mathewson (winner of 37 games that year). When Pfiester allowed a run in the bottom of the first inning and had two men on, Chance, aware that giving Mathewson more than a few runs' lead could be fatal, called in Brown. Mordecai extricated his mates from the situation without further damage.

In the top of the third, the Cubs suddenly struck at Mathewson. Tinker, whom Mathewson always called one of his toughest outs, led off with a triple, then scored the tying run on Kling's single. Brown sacrificed Kling to second, but Sheckard flied out. Mathewson then walked Evers and surrendered back-to-back doubles to Schulte and Chance, making it 4–1. The final score was 4–2, giving the Cubs their third straight pennant. Were Giant fans upset by the heartbreaking loss? Well, the Cubs needed a police escort to get out of the Polo Grounds and another one to get out of New York.

Pitching had again dominated an especially weak-hitting league (the National League batting average in 1908 was the lowest in its history, .239). For the Cubs Brown was 29–9 (most wins ever by a Cub pitcher in the twentieth century), and Reulbach 24–7, with Big Ed turning in one of baseball's one-of-a-kind feats on September 26, when he pitched both ends of a doubleheader against Brooklyn and came away with shutouts, 5–0 and 3–0. Other pitchers have won two complete games in one day, but only Reulbach delivered shutouts. The Cub ace allowed 5 hits and no walks in the opener and 3 hits and 1 walk in the closer. This Brooklyn team was ripe for a double plucking, for in 1908 they pop-gunned away to the lowest team batting average in modern National League history, .213. They were also Reulbach's favorite opponents—he beat them nine times that year, a record for one pitcher's mastery over one team in a season.

The Cubs managed one .300 hitter in this season of tepid offense, Evers, who came in at .300 on the button. The Chicago cast re-

Ed Reulbach, the only pitcher ever to throw shutouts on both ends of a doubleheader.

mained unchanged: Chance, Evers, Tinker, and Steinfeldt in the infield, Kling catching, and Schulte, Sheckard, and Slagle in the outfield, with Hofman the versatile utility man filling in wherever needed.

Detroit had repeated as American League champions and, led by the great Cobb, came into the World Series hoping to do better than they had the previous year, when the best they could do was a tie game. Well, they did do better, but not much, winning just one game.

Johnny Evers getting loose during
batting practice.

The opener went to the Cubs, 10–6. Reulbach had been whacked around, and the Cubs
went into the top of the ninth trailing 6–5
but then parlayed 6 singles and 2 stolen bases
into 5 runs.

In Game 2 the Cubs again used the big
inning, scoring six times in the eighth for a
6–1 victory, highlighted by Tinker's home
run, the first ever by a Cub in a World Series.
Overall was the winner, with a 4-hitter.

Detroit won Game 3, 8–3, beating Pfiester;
Cobb rapped 4 hits. After that, Chicago
pitching tightened the faucets and gave the
team its second straight world championship.
Brown pitched a 4-hit 3–0 shutout in Game
4, and Overall a 3-hit 2–0 blanker in the finale. The last game, played in Detroit,
showed once more that Tiger fans had thrown
in the towel; only 6,210 people attended, an

Three-Finger Brown.

39

Johnny Kling, ace catcher and pocket billiards champion.

Chance's men won 104 games but spent a frustrating summer pursuing the Pirates, who never faltered on their way to winning 110 games (which ties them with the 1927 Yankees for third-highest victory total in big-league history).

With the team batting .245, fourth best in the league, it was once again pitching that made Chicago a contender. Brown continued to have a firm, three-fingered grip on the distinction of being the National League's second-best pitcher (to Mathewson) with a 27–9 record, with 8 shutouts and a 1.31 ERA. Overall was 20–11, led with 9 shutouts, and had a 1.42 ERA; Reulbach was 19–10 and 1.78, and Pfiester 17–6 and 2.43. Reulbach set a team record with 14 straight wins, while Overall was the league strikeout leader with 205. (It would be fifty-eight years before another Cub pitcher—Ferguson Jenkins in 1967—reached the 200 mark in strikeouts.)

Backup catcher Pat Moran (1906–1909).

all-time-record low for a World Series game. The length of the game, one hour and twenty-five minutes, set another record, for World Series brevity.

Their second successive world championship topped off a most satisfying year for the Cubs, during which their regular-season attendance hit a new peak of 665,325, which would stand as a franchise record until 1923.

The Cubs failed to make it four in a row in 1909, but the failure was a splendid one—

Solly Hofman.

Their 104 wins notwithstanding, the Cubs might have done even better in 1909 had not Kling retired. Chicago's top catcher was an expert man with a pool cue and, during the winter of 1908 to 1909, had won the world pocket billiard title, a celebrated accomplishment in those years. Johnny decided to give up baseball and concentrate on his other game, for which Charles Murphy called him a "traitor," blaming Chicago's second-place finish on his desertion.

Replacing Kling was a tandem of Jimmy Archer, soon to become the regular, and Pat Moran. Another change took place in center field, where Hofman replaced the departed Slagle. Hofman, whose given name was Arthur and who was variously known as "Artie," "Solly," and "Circus Solly," led the team with a .285 average.

The Cubs 104–50 record in 1910 was almost identical to the 104–49 mark they

posted in 1909; but what was only second best in 1909 was a pennant-winning pace a year later, and an easy pennant too—they finished 13 games ahead of second-place New York.

Again the Cubs showed remarkable stability in their regular lineup; the only new face was actually a familiar one—Johnny Kling, who returned to baseball after losing his pocket billiard title. Johnny was now thirty-five years old and found himself splitting the catching duties with Archer. Otherwise, there they were as usual: Chance, Evers, and Tinker at their posts for an eighth consecutive year; Steinfeldt at third, and Sheckard, Hofman, and Schulte in the outfield. Schulte's 10 home runs were enough to make him the first Cub home-run king of the modern era. Hofman led the pennant winners with a .325 average, highest for a Cub regular since Steinfeldt's .327 in 1906.

With a slightly livelier ball in play now, the Cubs hit 34 home runs, more than any

Leonard ("King") Cole (1909–1912), whose career was tragically short.

Cub team ever had (all individual, team, and league records and accomplishments will now date to 1901, the beginning of the modern era) and good enough to lead the league. Earned run averages were affected accordingly, and while the Cub staff led for the fifth time in six years, this time it was with a 2.51 figure.

Brown again led the staff, posting a 25–13 record and 1.86 ERA. The surprise of Chance's mound crew was twenty-four-year-old rookie right-hander Leonard ("King") Cole, who broke in with a superb 20–4 record that was embellished with a 1.80 ERA. Cole's success helped offset the declines of Reulbach and Overall, each of whom slumped to 12 wins apiece, and of Pfiester, who won but 6. (Overall, not yet thirty years old, retired after the season because of an implacable dislike for Murphy. An attempted comeback in 1913 was unsuccessful.)

The Cubs went into the 1910 World Series against the Philadelphia Athletics under a se-

Heinie Zimmerman (1907–1916). His .307 average in 1911 was just a hint of his 1912 accomplishments.

vere handicap: Johnny Evers had broken his leg late in the season and could not play. Evers's place at second base was taken by Heinie Zimmerman, for several years a utility man (and the Cub third baseman of the future).

Even with Evers in the lineup, however, the Cubs probably would not have fared better against Connie Mack's A's, who were baseball's coming team, young and talented and about to do what the aging Cubs had just done—win four pennants in five years. Connie had superb talents, including second baseman Eddie Collins, third baseman Frank ("Home Run") Baker, shortstop Jack Barry, and pitchers Jack Coombs (a thirty-game winner that year), Chief Bender, and the veteran lefty Eddie Plank. Plank came up with a lame arm before the Series and was unable to pitch, leaving Mack with just two starters, but even this disadvantage failed to make the Athletics falter on their way to the championship.

The Series opened in Philadelphia, where the Athletics took both games, Bender beating Overall 4–1 and Coombs whipping Brown 9–3. The Series moved on to Chicago where, pitching with one day's rest, Coombs came back and beat Reulbach, 12–5.

A deficit of three games to none in a World Series is like being at the bottom of a deep well—the light is dim and the prospects even dimmer. Thanks to some late-inning heroics, the Cubs managed to stave off total annihilation by winning Game 4. Trailing 3–2 in the bottom of the ninth, Schulte hit a double, and Chance drove him home with a triple to tie the game. In the bottom of the tenth, Archer doubled and came home on Sheckard's single, giving Chicago (and Brown in relief) a 4–3 win. But these theatrics only prevented the humiliation of a sweep and postponed the inevitable, for the next day Coombs was back on the mound for the A's for the third time in six days. The A's broke open a 2–1 game with 5 runs in the top of the eighth and went on to defeat Brown 7–2, clinching the championship.

The most successful decade in Chicago Cubs history was over.

F·O·U·R

NEW FACES

THE debacle of the 1910 World Series, during which the Cubs were outscored 35–15, was both symbolic and significant for the team that had dominated the National League for the past five years.

The first serious erosions to the team came in the famous infield. A career's accumulation of injuries, including many painful beanings, which some people feel led to his death in 1924 at the age of forty-seven, reduced Chance's playing time in 1911 to just 31 games. "The Peerless Leader" (one of the skipper's nicknames; it was an era when appellatives often came in bouquets) was just about through as an active player.

The always high-strung Evers sat out most of the season with a nervous breakdown, Steinfeldt had been sold to Boston, with Kling following in midseason, Overall had retired, and Pfiester was released.

The Tinker-Evers-Chance combine had played together for eight years, an impres-

Johnny Evers *(left)* and Frank Chance *(right)*, with champion racing-car driver Barney Oldfield.

44

sively long tenure. Individually they were fine ball players, but as a double-play unit, they were overrated. Research done by New York sportswriter Charlie Segar revealed that from 1906 through 1909 the quaintly poeticized "trio of bear cubs" executed just 56 double

Vic Saier (1911–1917), who at the age of twenty replaced Chance as the Cubs' first baseman.

plays. So much for poetry as a guide to deucing a ground ball.

Replacing Chance at first base was Vic Saier, while Heinie Zimmerman, a notably heavy-handed fielder, filled in at second. (The error-prone Heinie redeemed himself with a .307 batting average.)

Chicago's most exciting player that year was Frank Schulte. The man known as "Wildfire" set a major-league record with 21 dingers, an extraordinary number for the time. (The record lasted only until 1915, when Philadelphia's Gavvy Cravath hit 24.) Schulte also became Chicago's first total-base leader with 308 and its second RBI champ with 121. In addition he set a team record

Frank ("Wildfire") Schulte, who led the league in home runs (21) and RBIs (121) in 1911.

with 21 triples, helping the Cubs to 101 three-baggers, still the club high.

Jimmy Sheckard established a new National League record with 147 bases on balls, a mark that stood until 1945, when Brooklyn's Eddie Stanky nudged past it by one. All this trotting down to first base gave Jimmy a head start on going around the bases, and he ended up leading the league with 121 runs scored.

Replacing Steinfeldt at third was Jimmy Doyle, who batted .282. Sadly, it was to be the thirty-year-old Doyle's only season with the Cubs; on February 1, 1912, he died of appendicitis.

The Cubs finished second in 1911, 7½ games behind the Giants. Brown was 21–11, a twenty-game winner for the sixth consecutive, and final time; Cole followed up his sensational rookie year with an 18–7 record, and Reulbach was 16–9.

Chicago's decline continued to be gentle rather than precipitous, as the team slipped to third place in 1912, their 91 victories giving them ninety or more for the ninth year in a row (no other National League team has had such sustained success). It was a year of sharp contrasts among some of the Cub personnel, ranging from sparkling success to dimming twilight and ending in noisy controversy.

The success belonged to Heinie Zimmerman, who put together a rousing Triple Crown season: .372 batting average, 14 home runs, 103 runs batted in. Having what later-day baseball people would call "a career year," Heinie also led the league in hits (207), doubles (41), slugging (.571), and total bases (318). He also led third basemen in errors with 35, the first of three straight years he would fumble his way to this unwanted distinction.

Another Cub who enjoyed his best year in 1912 was the veteran Evers, who checked in with a .341 batting average, a neon light on the ledger of a man whose lifetime average was .276.

The Cubs introduced a big winner to the league in rookie right-hander Larry Cheney,

a spitball artist who broke in with a 26–10 season. Another rookie righty was Jimmy Lavender, who was 16–13. Jimmy's big moment came against the Giants on July 8, 1912. New York's fine left-hander, Rube Marquard, had opened the season with 19 consecutive wins and was going for number 20 at the West Side Grounds. A large crowd, estimated at around 25,000, was in attendance to watch Lavender bring to an end what remains the longest individual one-season winning streak in baseball history, as the Cubs defeated Marquard and the Giants, 7–2.

Cheney and Lavender helped make up for the declines of Brown (5–6 and released after the season) and Cole, who was 1–2 before be-

Jimmy Doyle, a third baseman who played in 130 games for the Cubs in 1911.

The controversy came at the end of the season, when Charles Murphy fired Chance. The owner contended that the team's performance had been damaged by the manager's tolerance for excessive tippling among the players. Chance rose to the defense of his men, claiming they were sober and reliable. After that, the rhetoric grew hotter. Chance denounced his former employer with all the fervor of one freshly canned, calling Murphy a cheapskate, saying Charlie was unwilling to

Heinie Zimmerman, the Cubs' first batting champion. He won the Triple Crown in 1912.

ing traded to Pittsburgh with Solly Hofman in June. Cole, whose career had begun so brilliantly, was sadly doomed to premature death; he died of tuberculosis in January 1916, not yet thirty years old.

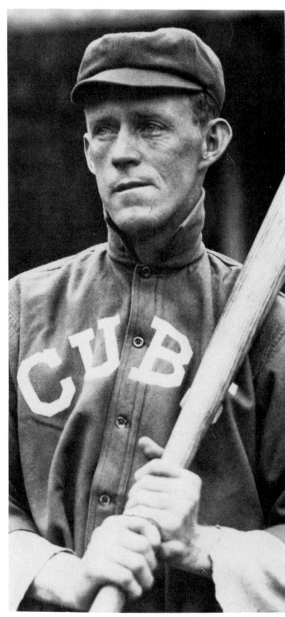

Johnny Evers batted .341 for the Cubs in 1912.

A twenty-game winner in his first three full seasons in the majors, Larry Cheney (1911–1915) went downhill quickly after that.

Brooklyn in July. That left only Evers and Schulte remaining from the glory years, and Johnny's number was coming up in a hurry.

Evers's moody, testy personality was not designed for managing a ball club. Normally a player like Evers, whose baseball acumen was widely acknowledged and respected, is virtually assured of a solid managerial career;

spend to improve either the team or the condition of the ballpark.

"In all the time I have been with this club," Chance said, "I have had to fight to get the players I wanted. Murphy has not spent one-third as much for players as have other magnates."

Murphy seemed to take the accusation as a compliment, saying, in reference to the other owners, "If they want to be suckers and pay it, they can, but I won't."

Soon after Chance's departure, Murphy appointed Evers manager. As soon as he heard about it, Johnny's famed DP partner and antagonist Joe Tinker asked to be traded. Murphy obliged him, and Joe was dealt to Cincinnati. Brown was gone, as were Chance and Tinker; Sheckard was sold to St. Louis in April 1913, and Reulbach was traded to

Jimmy Lavender (1912–1916), whose best year was his first, when he won 16 games.

Pitcher Harry McIntyre (1910–1912), who gave the Cubs a couple of effective seasons before hurting his arm.

The versatile Solly Hofman, who was traded with King Cole to Pittsburgh.

48

Joe and Mrs. Tinker, all set for a night on the town. Joe had asked to be traded when Johnny Evers was named manager of the Cubs.

and while he did later manage the Cubs again in 1921 and the White Sox in 1924, Johnny's inability to get along with his players shut him out of what might have been a managerial career of some substance.

Despite the dissension on the club, the Cubs earned another third-place finish in 1913. Zimmerman slipped to a .313 average, best on the squad, while Saier led the league and tied Schulte's record of 21 triples. Playing shortstop for Chicago for this one year was Al Bridwell, who as a New York Giant had lined the fateful single in 1908 on which Merkle had failed to touch second base.

Cheney turned in a good sophomore season (21–14), while right-hander Bert Humphries, acquired in the Tinker deal, was 16–4. Also on the staff that year, though slightly noticed, were big left-hander Jim ("Hippo") Vaughn, who was 5–1 and about to become the club ace, and right-hander Fred Toney, who pitched only seven games and was soon shipped to Cincinnati. Four years

Right-hander Lew Richie (1910–1913).

Al Bridwell (1913), the man who hit the famous single in 1908.

later these two would oppose each other in one of baseball's most celebrated mound duels.

After the 1913 season, Murphy decided to bounce Evers, setting into motion a chain of events that was to leave a lasting impact on Chicago Cub history.

Evers was only thirty-two years old and still a top-notch player; to get rid of his skipper, Murphy had to trade him. When Evers heard of this, he threatened to jump to the Federal League, the ill-fated third major league which was then being formed. The rest of the National League club owners, already gearing up to do battle with the newcomers (whom they viewed as brazen interlopers and worse) were appalled at the idea that one of the league's top stars was in effect being forced into the ranks of the outlaw league. So Murphy was summoned to a meeting in the office of league president John Tener (the former Cub player).

Present at the meeting was Charles Taft of Cincinnati, who had originally bankrolled Murphy in the Cub venture. Tener, Taft, and various league officials informed Murphy that baseball no longer needed his services. Murphy's dignity was comforted by approximately one-half million dollars, which Taft coughed up for Charley's 53 percent interest in the club. Taft then appointed Charles Thomas to run the club for him.

When all the dust had settled, Evers, who had been fired as manager, considered himself a free agent. So Johnny sold himself for $40,000 to the Boston Braves, whom he would help lead to a "miracle" pennant in 1914, the team climbing from last place on July 4.

Fred Toney (1911–1913), who defeated Hippo Vaughn in baseball's only double no-hitter.

Right-hander Bert Humphries (1913–1915), who was 16–4 in 1913.

In 1914, the embodiment of a bad idea, the Federal League, set up shop in eight cities, Chicago among them, giving the city three teams. This self-anointed major league lasted for just two seasons, during which time it put some bruises on the Cubs, cutting the older team's attendance in half from what it had been in 1913 (the White Sox also suffered a considerable drop at the gate). But the Chicago Federal League team, which was known as the Whales and was managed by Joe Tinker, would leave behind one of the city's enduring baseball legacies.

The Cub manager in 1914 was Hank O'Day, a man who traveled one of baseball's most curious career paths. He had originally come to the major leagues as a pitcher with Toledo of the American Association in 1884, later playing in the National League with Washington and New York. He retired as a

player in 1890 and the next year made his debut as an umpire. In 1912 he gave up umpiring to take over as manager of the Cincinnati Reds, a job he held for just one season. In 1914 he became manager of the Cubs, and after a fourth-place finish, he was fired, whereupon he returned to umpiring and remained in that capacity until his retirement in 1927. It was umpire O'Day, of course, who had made the historic "out" call on Fred Merkle at the Polo Grounds on September 23, 1908.

The most notable point of interest for the Cubs in 1914 was the emergence of Vaughn

John K. Tener, Chicago pitcher (1888–1889), governor of Pennsylvania, National League president—and the man who helped edge Charles Murphy out of baseball.

Bresnahan officiated over a dreary losing season, the Cubs finishing fourth, 3½ games out of last place. Vaughn turned in another big season (20–12), but Cheney slipped to 8–9 and in August was traded to the Dodgers.

A couple of pitching exploits highlighted the Cubs' otherwise forgettable season. On

Charles Murphy, the Cubs' controversial owner, who had his team pulled out from under him.

Roger Bresnahan (1900, 1913–1915). He managed the club in 1915. He is probably best remembered today as the man who invented shin guards for catchers, but it was his talent on the field that got him into the Hall of Fame.

as an ace, the beginning of what was to be the greatest career of any Cub left-hander. Known as "Hippo" for the six-foot two-inch 215-pound shadow he cast, Vaughn had had earlier trials with the New York Yankees and Washington Senators. In August 1913 he was acquired by the Cubs from Kansas City. In 1914 he punched out a 21–13 record, while Larry Cheney made it three twenty-game seasons in a row with a 20–18 mark.

The skipper in 1915 was Roger Bresnahan, a big-league catcher for sixteen years, the last two as a part-timer with the Cubs. Formerly a player-manager with the Cardinals, Bresnahan is most remembered as the man who first wore shin guards behind the plate (around 1907), but there was obviously more to Bresnahan than that; it wasn't shin guards that got him elected to the Hall of Fame in 1945.

After the 1915 season, the Federal League folded its tents and drifted off to nestle among the footnotes of baseball history. One thing, however, was left behind—Weeghman Field, renamed Cubs Park in 1916, and in 1926, in deference to the man who owned the club, Wrigley Field.

Built to house the Chicago Whales, Weeghman Field was one of the premier parks in the Federal League. Originally built with a capacity of 14,200, it underwent various renovations through the years. In 1923 the grandstand was moved back several feet to enlarge seating capacity to 20,000. After the 1926 season, the field was double-decked from the right-field corner to the left, construction that increased accommodations to 40,000. In

Outfielder Wilbur Good (1911–1915). His best was a .272 average in 1914.

June 17 nondescript right-hander Zip Zabel turned in baseball's longest relief stint: 18⅓ innings of a 19-inning 4–3 victory over Brooklyn. And on August 31 Jimmy Lavender, muddling through a 10–16 year, turned in the first complete nine-inning no-hitter by a Cub pitcher in the modern era, smothering the Giants 9–0. (Earlier, on June 11, 1904, Bob Wicker had held the Giants hitless for nine innings, allowed a hit in the tenth, and went on to win in twelve, 1–0. On July 31, 1910, Len Cole had thrown a seven-inning, 4–0 no-hitter against the Cardinals in a game called in order to allow the teams to catch a train.) It would be forty years before another Cub pitcher hurled a victorious no-hitter.

Former New York Giant outfield star Red Murray played part of the 1915 season for the Cubs.

A photograph (ca. 1915) of the exterior of Weeghman Field, later to be called Wrigley Field.

1937 new outfield stands were built, altering dimensions that had been 364 feet to left, 436 to center, and 321 to right, to those that remain to this day: 355 to left, 400 to center, and 353 to right.

Through the years the tradition-rich old ballparks have one by one succumbed to obsolescence and been abandoned. Such places as Ebbets Field, the Polo Grounds, Sportsman's Park, Shibe Park, Crosley Field, Forbes Field, and others now belong to history alone. But a few of the old parks have remained, and none with more untiring and changeless charm than Wrigley Field, a ballpark built to absorb time and history and yet remain young.

For years Wrigley Field was known for be-

ing the only major-league facility without lights, a distinction that came to an end in 1988. Today, the most celebrated characteristic of the field is its ivy-covered brick walls, which add a pastoral air to a game which, after all, did grow up on the meadows and pastures of rural America. The analogy sometimes comes to life, as when some vexed outfielder has to search for a batted ball that has lodged itself in the vines, much as his forebears once upon a time had to beat the tall grass that had swallowed a ball at the rim of their unfenced playing field. In Wrigley the wellspring traditions go on, relaxed and undimmed.

Charles Weeghman, for whom the field was

originally named, was a well-heeled Chicagoan who had bankrolled the Chicago Whales. Unlike most of the Federal League owners, Weeghman was anxious to remain in baseball when the league folded. Deciding he wanted to run the Cubs, Weeghman found a willing seller in Charles Taft, who had shown little interest in the franchise. Putting together a syndicate of ten investors (including himself), each of whom kicked in $50,000, Weeghman bought the team from Taft and had himself installed as the front man. One of the other investors was chewing-gum magnate William Wrigley, who came in quietly but gradually began picking up more and more of the club's stock and taking greater interest in its affairs.

After the purchase was completed, Weeghman's first decision was to move the team from the West Side Grounds to the new park at Clark and Addison streets.

Weeghman's next move was to try to return some old-time flavor to the team; he hired Joe Tinker to manage in 1916. The old shortstop thus became the fifth manager in five years and the fourth straight to serve just one year—Joe bit the dust after the team finished fifth with a 67–86 record, the Cubs' worst since 1901.

The only bit of Cub glory that year came from outfielder Cy Williams, who led the league with 12 home runs. Cy would lead in home runs three more times, but it would be while wearing the uniform of the Phillies, to whom he was traded in December 1917.

The Cubs led in errors in 1916 with 286, the shortstop being the most glaring offender, with 89 slip ups. Chuck Wortman played

Weeghman Field in 1915, home of the Chicago Whales of the Federal League. It became the Cubs' home ballpark in 1916.

Cy Williams (1912–1917), who had his best years with the Phillies, for whom he played until 1930.

The Cubs played a little better in 1917 but still finished fifth again. The year produced the most remorseless pitching duel in baseball history. On May 2 Vaughn drew the assignment against old teammate Fred Toney, now with the visiting Cincinnati Reds. Both men were big winners that year, Vaughn 23–13, Toney 24–16. On May 2, 1917, they locked arms and created for themselves a unique place in baseball history.

For nine innings each man pitched scoreless no-hit ball, the only time in major-league

sixty-nine games at short and made 32 errors, while a .201 batting average made him an all-around dubious character. But compared to Eddie Mulligan, Chuck had a banner year. Playing fifty-eight games at short, Mulligan committed 40 errors and batted a feathery .153.

The last links to better days were severed that year when Schulte was traded to Pittsburgh in July and Zimmerman to New York in August.

The Cubs' sixth manager in six years was Fred Mitchell, who broke the revolving-door pattern by remaining for four years. Mitchell had pitched for the Red Sox, Athletics, Phillies, and Dodgers at the turn of the century with modest success and was coaching for the Braves when he accepted the Chicago job.

Fred Mitchell, who managed the Cubs from 1917 to 1920.

On Labor Day, September 4, 1916, Christy Matthewson (then managing the Reds) and Three-Finger Brown (who had returned to the Cubs for a last brief hurrah) were matched, sentimentally, for one last game, the final one of each man's career. Matthewson staggered through a 10–8 victory, the 373d of his career, a win total later matched by Grover Cleveland Alexander for most in National League history. This ad appeared in the *Chicago Daily News*.

history that both starters have done this. Then, with one out in the top of the tenth, Cincinnati's Larry Kopf rolled a single into right field. After a second out was made, Hal Chase hit a high line drive to right-center that Cy Williams should have handled but did not. The error sent Kopf around to third. The next batter was Jim Thorpe, the incomparable athlete who had dominated the 1912 Olympic games and was now trying his hand at big-league ball. Thorpe, who was better at the decathalon than he was at hitting the curveball, tapped a high bouncer in front of the plate. Vaughn moved in on the ball as Kopf headed down the line. Aware of

Thorpe's blinding speed, Vaughn decided to throw home to get Kopf. The ball was apparently there in time, but catcher Art Wilson muffed it. A bit of lenient scoring credited Thorpe with a single, and thus the famous "double no-hitter" ended with Vaughn giving up 2 hits in a 1–0 loss (Toney completed his no-hitter in the bottom of the tenth).

Vic Saier had broken his leg early in the season, creating a need for a first baseman. The man the Cubs obtained to plug the gap was none other than Fred Merkle. He had been traded by the Giants to the Dodgers the year before, and it was from Brooklyn that the Cubs obtained the man who will always

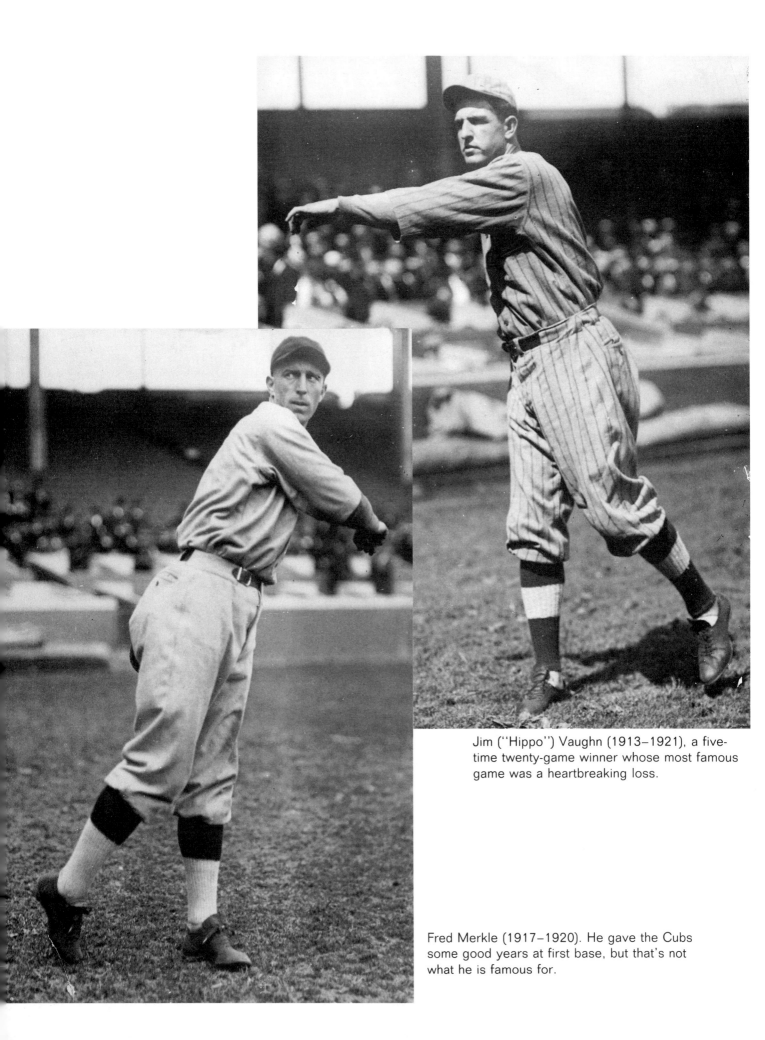

Jim ("Hippo") Vaughn (1913–1921), a five-time twenty-game winner whose most famous game was a heartbreaking loss.

Fred Merkle (1917–1920). He gave the Cubs some good years at first base, but that's not what he is famous for.

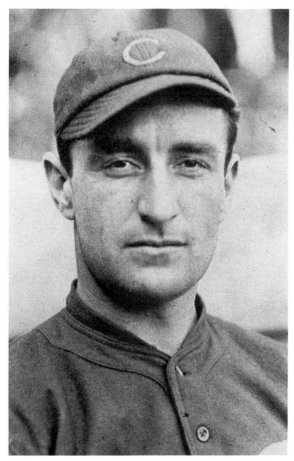

The Dublin-born Jimmy Archer (1909–1917).

itary service or war-related industries. In addition, baseball was ordered to close down on Labor Day, with a special grace period permitted for the playing of the World Series. With the abruptly curtailed schedule, teams averaged around 126 games each in 1918.

With one conspicuous exception, the Cubs were not hit as hard by the national situation as most teams. The exception, though, was none other than Grover Cleveland Alexander, the league's top pitcher and the only one in its annals to rank with the great Christy Mathewson. They occupy twin spots at the top of the National League victory scroll, with 373 apiece.

On December 11, 1917, Cub fans had been delighted to hear of their team's acquisition of Alex from the Phillies for two players and cash rumored to be around $55,000—heavy money for the time. Along with Alex came his favorite catcher, Bill Killefer.

figure so prominently in their history. Always a steady player, Merkle gave the Cubs four good years at first base.

The acquisition of Merkle maintained the curious connection the Cubs continued to have with the most famous game in their history. Al Bridwell, who had delivered the seemingly game-winning hit for the Giants on September 23, 1908, had played shortstop for Chicago in 1913, and Hank O'Day, the umpire who had made the courageous, and correct, ruling that day, had managed the Cubs in 1914. And now here was Merkle himself, playing first base for the team to whose benefit he had committed one of baseball's most celebrated blunders.

The country had been at war since April 1917, but not until a year later did the conflict affect major-league rosters. In June the provost marshall issued a "work-or-fight" order, the purpose of which was to move all able-bodied men of draft age into either mil-

The great Grover Cleveland Alexander (1918–1926).

60

The thirty-year-old Alexander had been dazzling the league since 1911, ringing up a 190–88 record, and in his previous three years had posted win totals of 31, 33, and 30. According to one story, the Phillies had been induced to part with their ace because they feared he was going to be drafted. Whether the story was true or not, Alex pitched just three times for the Cubs in the spring of 1918 before being plucked for military service.

The man responsible for the hefty expenditure for Alexander was William Wrigley, who had recently taken control of the club. Using the leverage of his directorship and the assets gained from his chewing-gum fortune, Wrigley had gradually taken over and by 1921 was sole owner, establishing a line of familial ownership that would last until 1981. Wrigley also helped move into place another high-pedigree baseball line when he hired as Cubs vice-president (later president) William Veeck, Sr., whose son Bill would himself later become a big-league club owner and build a reputation as one of the game's most gifted and entertaining promoters and showmen.

Despite the loss of Alexander, Mitchell's Cubs were the surprise team in the league, taking over first place in early June and going on to win the pennant by 10½ games over second-place New York. Playing 129 games in the abbreviated season, the Cubs were 84–45, a .651 winning percentage, which no Cub team since has bettered.

Credit for tuning an also-ran team into winners was given largely to rookie shortstop Charlie Hollocher. The twenty-two-year-old Hollocher filled what had been the team's most troublesome position with sparkle and verve, batting .316 and leading the league with 161 hits. Merkle's .297 average was next best on the team.

The Cubs ran three top pitchers across the mounds of the National League that year—Vaughn (22–10), George ("Lefty") Tyler (19–9), and Claude Hendrix (19–7). No team in the league came close to matching this trio. Vaughn was the ERA leader with a 1.74 mark, while he and Tyler each pitched 8

Bill Killefer (1918–1921), Cub manager from 1921 to 1925, and Alexander's favorite catcher.

shutouts. Tyler, who had been a member of the Boston Brave staff that pitched the team to its "miracle" pennant in 1914, was obtained in a deal with the Braves.

Chicago's opponents in the 1918 World Series were the Boston Red Sox, just completing their own reign in baseball's version of a dynasty—four pennants in seven years. Rather weak on offense, the Red Sox had an excellent starting rotation in Carl Mays, Sam Jones, "Bullet" Joe Bush, and left-hander

Charlie Hollocher (1918–1924), the rookie shortstop who led the league with 161 hits in 1918.

Babe Ruth. The twenty-three-year-old Ruth was just beginning to make the transition from ace pitcher to star slugger. Pitching less and playing more, he had worked to a 13–7 record, played in ninety-five games (some at first base, some in the outfield), batted .300, and tied for the home-run lead with 11. Ruth, who was to pitch brilliantly in the Series, was also Boston's most dangerous hitter.

Travel restrictions required that the first three games be played in Chicago, with the remainder to be played in Boston. Trying to attract the largest attendance possible, the Chicago games were played in Comiskey Park, the only time the Cubs have ever played a home game at Comiskey. There was recent precedent for this kind of commercial maneuver: in 1915 and 1916, the pennant-winning Red Sox had played their Series home games not at Fenway Park but at the more commodious home field of the Boston Braves.

The 1918 edition was the tamest World Series in history, with a combined total of just 19 runs scored. The Cubs outscored the Sox, 10–9, but Boston's production was more timely, and they won the Series in six games.

Claude Hendrix (1916–1920). His 19–7 record in 1918 was his only winning season.

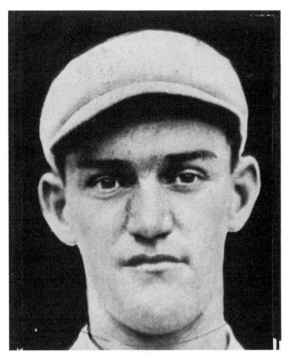

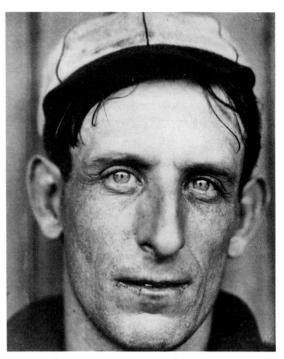

George (''Lefty'') Tyler (1918–1921). He topped the league with 8 shutouts in 1918.

Utility infielder Rollie Zeider (1916–1918).

Hippo Vaughn, the best left-hander in Cub history.

Phil Douglas (1915, 1917–1919).

tom of the third when right-fielder Max Flack muffed a line drive with two out and runners on second and third.

Their inability to back up their good pitching with any semblance of hitting made it a depressing Series for the Cub players. Nor did they receive much comfort from their Series shares. With most of the country concentrating on the cannon fire and casualty lists in France, attendance was below expectations; also, this was the first year that first-division teams received shares of Series receipts. Consequently, the losers' shares came to a mere $671 apiece.

Mitchell brought his troops in third in 1919, a season reduced to 140 games because

In the opener, played on September 5, Ruth slipped past Vaughn, 1–0, a game that set the Series pattern. The Cubs tied it in Game 2, 3–0, with Tyler pitching the shutout. (The Cubs scored all their runs in the bottom of the second, the biggest one-inning outburst of the Series.) Vaughn was back in Game 3 with one day's rest and again had hard luck, losing to Carl Mays, 2–1.

The Series then moved on to Boston, where Mitchell continued his scheme of starting only his left-handers, Vaughn and Tyler. Ruth beat Tyler 3–2 in Game 4. It was in this game that Babe set his record for consecutive scoreless innings in World Series play, dating back to the 1916 Series, running it to $29\frac{2}{3}$ before the Cubs broke through in the top of the eighth. (The record lasted until 1961, when it was broken by the Yankees' Whitey Ford.) Vaughn pitched another strong game the next day, and this time came away a winner, 3–0. But then the Red Sox wrapped it up in another close one, Mays beating Tyler, 2–1, with the Boston runs scoring in the bot-

Outfielder Les Mann (1916–1919).

A full house at Weeghman Field.

the owners were uncertain about the public's postwar interest in baseball (the owners need not have worried, as attendance was up all over).

Vaughn turned in what had, by now, become his standard year—21–14. Grover Cleveland Alexander returned from the war, shattered beyond repair after suffering shell shock. He came back alcoholic and epileptic but was still steady on the mound, which became virtually the only reassuring place on earth for him. He was 16–11, leading the league with a 1.72 ERA and 9 shutouts. The Chicago staff posted a collective 2.21 ERA, leading the league for the ninth time since 1901. But two of 1918's big winners slipped badly, Hendrix to 10–14 and Tyler to 2–2.

The talk in Chicago in 1919 was not about the Cubs but the White Sox, whose superb team had won the pennant. After a World Series performance against Cincinnati that trailed odors matching those of Chicago's famous stockyards, there was more and more talk about the White Sox, none of it complimentary. By the end of the 1920 season, the Black Sox scandal, which had been festering all summer, exploded. It was a most sensitive

time for baseball, which had not only a World Series swindle on its hands but also rumors and allegations from various sources about players betting on games and in some instances helping to arrange the final score. Star players including Hal Chase and Heinie Zimmerman (both then with the New York Giants) were accused of tickling ground balls they should have been grabbing. Other players were accused of offering bribes to their colleagues. Public faith in the game began to wane.

Fearing for their investments, the owners acted to restore the integrity of baseball. Urged on by William Wrigley, they hired a czar to run their game in whom they vested virtually unlimited powers, Chicago federal judge Kenesaw Mountain Landis, as tough and unforgiving a hangman as ever sat on a judgment seat. By action and by edict, he set about cleaning up baseball, striking fear into the heart of any would-be miscreant.

The judge also received some help on the field, where fan interest was being freshly excited by the sizzling line drives and high-flying blasts of the lively ball. It was, in effect, a whole new ball game.

THE BOOM-TIME DECADE

IN his final year as manager, Fred Mitchell brought the Cubs in fifth in 1920, but their finish was no reflection on Grover Cleveland Alexander's performance. In a season reminiscent of those before the war, Alex was 27–14, leading in ERA (1.91), strikeouts (173), complete games (33), and innings pitched (363, a team record). With Vaughn at 19–16, the two aces accounted for 46 of the team's 75 wins.

The Cubs were also tainted by baseball's scandals. On August 31 William Veeck received word that his starting pitcher that day, Claude Hendrix, had allegedly bet $5,000 against his own team. Hendrix was immediately scratched. Although the pitcher denied the story, the Cubs felt the circumstantial evidence was persuasive. The story was released to the press, and Hendrix was through. The Cubs released him in February, and at the age of thirty-two, his career was over.

Shortstop Charlie Hollocher batted .319 but played in only eighty games, missing the rest of the time with a stomach ailment. It was the beginning of a pattern for the Cubs' star. After a medical examination that found nothing wrong, Charlie insisted he was ill and suffering. He gave the team two more complete seasons but then pleaded illness in 1923, playing in sixty-six games; in 1924 he played in just seventy-six games, again claiming an illness that no doctor could identify. He retired after that season, at the age of twenty-eight. At the age of forty-four, in 1940, he committed suicide.

Years later, Burleigh Grimes, who had played against him, remembered Hollocher as "the best shortstop I ever saw, after Honus Wagner. He claimed he was sick, but nobody believed him, which I guess didn't make him feel any better. He was a very intense guy. Some people said he had emotional problems that he couldn't handle and it tied him up in knots. I guess we'll never know."

Grover Cleveland Alexander, warming up.

William Veeck.

beautiful piece of land lying in the San Pedro Channel just south of Los Angeles. Catalina remained the team's spring base until 1952, when the camp was moved to Mesa, Arizona.

Killefer's boys hit the ball harder in 1922 than they did in 1921, but so did the rest of the league—the Cubs' .293 average was bettered by four other clubs, the same four that finished ahead of the fifth-place Chicagoans. That year five regulars hit above .300: outfielder Hack Miller, .352 (highest ever for a Cub rookie); Hollocher, .340; catcher Bob O'Farrell, .324; Grimes, .354; and outfielder Barney Friberg, .311. Grimes and Miller were second and third in league batting but were never really in the race, as the man at the top was the Cardinals' Rogers Hornsby, at .401. Charlie Hollocher was never sharper than that year; in 592 official at-bats in 152 games,

Mitchell was fired after the 1920 season, and his replacement, something of a surprise, was Johnny Evers. This ghost of glories past had not mellowed with age, and early in July ace left-hander Hippo Vaughn (whose own disposition probably was not improved by his 3–11 record) packed up and went home rather than work for Evers. Big Jim never returned, not even when Evers was given the boot a month later and was replaced by Bill Killefer, whose catching career was just about over. The team finished seventh, up to that point the worst finish of any Cub outfit in the twentieth century.

The influence of the lively ball was beginning to be felt in the Chicago lineup, with the club turning out four .300 hitters in rookie first baseman Ray Grimes (.321) and outfielders Turner Barber (.314) George Maisel (.310), and Max Flack (.301). The team average was a new high, .292, and their 1,226 singles are still the Cub record.

By 1922 the Cubs were taking their spring training in a most enviable location: William Wrigley's Catalina Island, a languorously

Outfielder first baseman Turner Barber (1917–1922). He was a .314 hitter in 1921.

two clubs (49), and most hits in a game, two clubs (51). For the Cubs the 26 runs and the 14-run inning remain highs in team history. Remarkably, the Phillies used just two pitchers in the game; the Cubs, five.

Killefer and his team finished fourth in 1923, and Cub fans appreciated the effort, setting a new team attendance record with 703,705 paid admissions. The Cubs were handicapped that year by the loss of two of

Outfielder Max Flack (1916–1922). Max batted .300 in 1920 and 1921, but he is most remembered for having been traded to the Cardinals for Cliff Heathcote between games of a doubleheader.

he struck out just five times, a league record for fewest strikeouts for a player in 150 or more games.

Chicago's game of the year, and the game that most represented the decade's ludicrously high batting averages, was played at Wrigley Field between the Cubs and Phillies on August 25, 1922. The Cubs scored 10 runs in the bottom of the third, then 14 more in the bottom of the fourth, at which time the score was 25–6. But the Phillies tore loose for 8 runs in the top of the eighth and 6 more in the top of the ninth and had the bases loaded when the last out of the 26–23 Chicago victory was made.

The record book got a good scrubbing that afternoon, including a couple of major rewritings that still stand: most runs in a game,

Charlie Deal, who covered third base for the Cubs from 1916 through 1921, when he retired at the age of thirty.

William Wrigley, holding the rich man's lifeline. The Cubs enjoyed spring training on Wrigley's Catalina Island from 1922 to 1952.

greatest of Cub catchers and one of the best of all time.

At the age of thirty-six, Alexander was still a big winner, turning in a 22–12 season, during which he walked just 30 men in 305 innings, at one stretch going 51 consecutive innings without walking a batter. Alex was backed up by right-hander Vic Aldridge, who was 16–9.

The Cubs hit 90 home runs, setting a new team record; they also led the league with 181 stolen bases, most for a Cub team in the lively ball era. (Never a club with a propensity for

Hack Miller (1922–1925). Son of a circus strong-man, Hack himself was considered the strongest man in baseball and would occasionally entertain the fans with weight-lifting exhibitions. Fielding deficiencies helped abbreviate his career.

their stars for much of the summer: Grimes, hitting .329 at the time, suffered a slipped disc in June, a misfortune that all but ended his career; and Hollocher began disappearing from the lineup with his mysterious stomach ailments, batting .342 in sixty-six games.

The Cubs had other .300 hitters in third baseman Friberg (.318), outfielders Jigger Statz (.319) and Hack Miller (.301), and catcher Bob O'Farrell (.319). As good as O'Farrell was, the Cubs already had someone who would soon replace him—Gabby Hartnett,

Shown here in a Giants uniform, Bob O'Farrell (1915–1925, 1934) was an outstanding catcher, but the Cubs also had Gabby Hartnett.

Charlie Grimm, shortstop Rabbit Maranville, and left-hander Wilbur Cooper.

Although Aldridge and Grantham went on to help the Pirates to pennants in 1925 and 1927, the trade had long-range benefits for the Cubs, for in Grimm they acquired a man who would play many roles in the organization for years to come. Always a favorite of the Wrigleys, Grimm was personable and witty (he was known as "Jolly Cholly"), with a zesty appetite for humor. Twenty-six years old when he joined the Cubs, Charlie had played briefly for the Athletics and Cardinals, then put in five full seasons with the Pirates, during which time he developed a reputation as one of the finest fielding first basemen in baseball. Steady rather than spectacular at the plate, he was primarily a contact hitter, concluding his twenty-year career in 1936 with a .290 lifetime average.

the stolen base, they have led the league in steals only three times since 1920.)

The 1924 Cubs finished fifth; nevertheless, for the second year in a row, they set a new club attendance record, cranking the turn-stiles 716,922 times. An injury to O'Farrell gave Hartnett his opportunity behind the plate, where he would remain for fifteen years. Hollocher was about through; his replacement, Earl ("Sparky") Adams, gave the team some excellent service in the infield over the next few years. Second baseman George Grantham was a .316 hitter, but his 44 errors made him expendable, and on October 27, 1924, the Cubs packaged him, pitcher Vic Aldridge, and first baseman Al Niehaus and sent them to the Pirates for first baseman

Barney Friberg, who played outfield and infield for the Cubs from 1919 to 1925.

Outfielder Arnold (''Jigger'') Statz (1922–1925).

Charles Leo (''Gabby'') Hartnett (1922–1940), greatest of all Cub catchers.

Right-hander Vic Aldridge (1917–1924), who gave the Cubs some good years before being traded to the Pirates in a package for Charlie Grimm, Rabbit Maranville, and Wilbur Cooper.

Earl ("Sparky") Adams (1922–1927), who put in time at second, third, and short for the Cubs.

The combined managing skills of Killefer, Maranville, and Gibson brought the Cubs home in a spot they had never occupied before, last place. Irked by the abysmal 1925 season and riled by the antics of Maranville (who was waived to Brooklyn after the season) and several of the other players, Veeck set out to restructure the club and install a manager who would bring discipline and direction.

A former newspaperman, Veeck had contacts throughout baseball. That fall, when he began hunting for a new manager, he kept

With Grimm and Maranville, the Cubs received a heady injection of personality, for Rabbit was one of the game's all-time pranksters and mischief makers. A thirteen-year veteran when he came to the Cubs, Rabbit could play shortstop, but his off-the-field antics would soon make intolerable demands on William Veeck's sense of humor.

When Killefer resigned in midseason, Veeck appointed Maranville manager, a mistake that grew more obvious with each passing day. After his first win as skipper, Rabbit went out to celebrate in New York's speakeasies and ended the evening brawling with a cab driver who did not appreciate not having been tipped. Rabbit spilled a bucket of water on John Seys, the traveling secretary, and, in the peccadillo that finally got him fired, went dancing through a Pullman car one night splashing the occupants with baptismal jets from a spittoon. Coach George Gibson took the reins for the club's final twenty-six games.

Charlie Grimm (1925–1936), first baseman, manager, and all-around Chicago Cub institution.

The mischievous Rabbit Maranville (1925). He played in the big leagues for twenty-three years, but for Chicago one was enough.

hearing the most complimentary reports about the skipper of the Louisville club of the American Association, Joe McCarthy. McCarthy, he heard, was a sound baseball man, a strict disciplinarian who at the same time had a knack for getting along with his players. If a player was disruptive or did not fit in, Joe would get rid of him.

"He was a master psychologist," said Tommy Henrich of McCarthy, who managed Henrich in Joe's later, more famous tenure with the Yankees. "We were in awe of him, all of us, and that included Gehrig and DiMaggio and everybody else. Everybody."

The one handicap McCarthy brought with him to Chicago was never having played in the major leagues. A career minor leaguer, Joe had spent fifteen years in baseball's outer reaches, most of it as a second baseman who generally poked the ball in the .260 range. So when the thirty-eight-year-old Pennsylvania-born Irishman took over the Cubs, he found among them some smirking skeptics who considered him a "bush leaguer."

The first serious challenge to McCarthy's attempt to bring his brand of dignified law and order to the squad came from the man who was not only the team's biggest "name" player but one of baseball's living legends, Grover Cleveland Alexander.

During a team meeting early in the season, McCarthy was going over a change in signs, necessitated by the trading of a Cub player to the team the Cubs were playing that day. McCarthy was concerned about the man being able to steal the catcher's signs from second base. Alexander, whose drinking problem had steadily worsened, shuffled into the meeting late and took a chair at the rear. When he learned the subject under discussion, he said with a foolish grin, "Not to worry. If that fellow was ever going to get to second base, McCarthy wouldn't have traded him."

There was laughter. McCarthy smiled tightly.

"Alex meant no harm," Joe said in an interview years later. "He was really a nice fellow, and I liked him. He lived by the rules, but they were always Alex's rules."

On June 22, 1926, Alexander was waived to the Cardinals, whom he helped to win pennants in that year and in 1928. But McCarthy had made his point, and it was not lost on the rest of the team—if Alexander could be disposed of, then McCarthy, with the backing of ownership, was in command.

It was on the advice of the new manager that the Cubs made a key pickup in the autumn of 1925. The Giants had farmed outfielder Lewis ("Hack") Wilson to the American Association in 1925 and through a clerical oversight left him unprotected in

Joe McCarthy, Cub manager from 1926 through 1930.

physique could take it, he drank hard and played hard.

McCarthy was strict, but he was no puritan. He recognized Hack's strengths as well as his weaknesses, and as long as those weaknesses did not impair the strengths, as long as

It's spring training 1925 and Grover Cleveland Alexander is posing before the hills of Catalina Island.

baseball's postseason draft of minor leaguers. McCarthy urged Veeck to draft Wilson, and so for $7,500 the Cubs took possession of the man who a few years later would turn in the single most thunderous offensive season in their history.

Wilson stood five feet six inches and weighed 190 muscular pounds. His nickname was derived from the name of a prominent wrestler of the time, George Hackenschmidt. One of baseball's strongest men, Wilson was a genial, sweet-natured man with a serious weakness for liquor. For as long as his robust

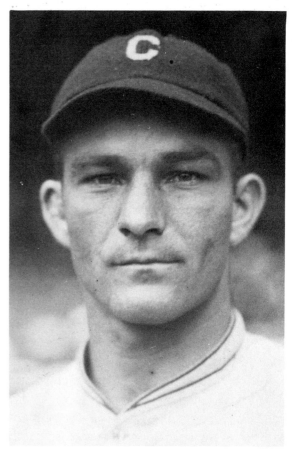

He looks strong, and he was. Hack Wilson (1926–1931) led the league in home runs in four of his six years in Chicago.

a hard-hitting infielder with Cleveland for five years, then had been sent to the minors because of a sore arm. McCarthy urged Veeck to acquire him, and in early June Stephenson joined the club, beginning eight years of tornado hitting.

In McCarthy's first year, the team climbed to fourth place, just 7 games out of first. The roly-poly, fun-loving Wilson popped 21 homers to lead the league, while batting .321 and driving in 109 runs, the first Cub to drive in more than 100 since Zimmerman in 1912. Stephenson, in his half year, was a .338 hitter, and Sparky Adams hit .309. On the mound McCarthy got an 18–17 season from rookie right-hander Charlie Root, who was beginning the longest career of any pitcher in Cub history (sixteen years). Right-hander Guy Bush was 13–9.

a man was ready to play and play hard, the skipper would look the other way. Also, Wilson was one of his all-time favorites.

"A lot of guys picked on Hack because he was small," McCarthy said, "but Hack showed them it was a mistake. He knew how to punch, and when he landed one, it was all over."

Another new man on the 1926 Cubs was outfielder Riggs Stephenson. Riggs had been

Riggs Stephenson (1926–1934). His .336 batting average for his nine seasons in Chicago is the highest in team history.

unassisted triple play, in the first game of a May 30 Memorial Day doubleheader against the Pirates. Jimmy pulled this most economically sound of baseball defensive plays by snaring a line drive off the bat of Paul Waner, stepping on second to retire Paul's brother Lloyd, and then tagging Clyde Barnhart, who was running from first. A week later Jimmy was traded to the Phillies for right-hander Hal Carlson, with rookie Woody English taking over at short.

The good hitting of Grimm (.311), Wilson (.318), Stephenson (.344), outfielder Earl Webb (.301), English (.290), Hartnett (.294), and Adams (.292, with a club-record 165 singles) made things interesting at Wrigley Field that summer and drew another record attendance mark of 1,159,168, making the Cubs

Utility infielder Clyde Beck (1926–1930).

McCarthy's invigorated team set a new club attendance mark—885,063. It wouldn't last long.

In 1927 the Cubs again finished fourth, after having led the league as late as the third week in August, but a September nosedive plunged them into fourth, 8½ games out.

On May 17 of that year, they played what remains the longest game in Cub history, a 22-inning, 4–3 victory over Boston. Just three days before, they had gone 18 innings in beating Boston, 7–2, with Bush going the distance. On May 30 Cub shortstop Jimmy Cooney executed the National League's last

Left-hander Percy Jones (1920–1922, 1925–1928). A 12–7 record in 1926 was his best showing.

Right-hander Guy Bush (1923–1934).

rates for Sparky Adams. A relentlessly aggressive player, the twenty-eight-year-old Cuyler had had some outstanding seasons for Pittsburgh but had then fallen into disfavor with manager Donie Bush, who had gone so far as to bench his star for the last two months of the 1927 season.

With Cuyler, Stephenson, and Wilson, the Cubs now had what is probably the strongest outfield in their history. Cuyler batted what was for him a disappointing .285, Stephenson .324, and Wilson .313, with Hack's 31 homers leading the league for the third straight time.

McCarthy's ace that year was right-hander Perce ("Pat") Malone, a tough, hard-throwing, hard-drinking character who, like Wilson, won the skipper's heart. Wilson and

Jimmy Cooney (1926–1927), who executed the National League's last unassisted triple play.

the first National League team to draw more than one million customers (this was the year the field was double-decked).

Wilson hit 30 home runs, setting a new club record and leading the league for the second year in a row, while driving in 129 runs. On the mound it was all Charlie Root, the tough right-hander having his finest season with a 26–15 record. Charlie started thirty-six games and relieved in twelve; his forty-eight appearances led the league. (It was not uncommon for an ace pitcher to lead in appearances in this era, before the advent of relief specialists.)

The Cubs made a strong run for the brass ring in 1928, coming up 4 games short as they finished third. They were abetted now by the superb all-around talents of Hazen ("Kiki") Cuyler, who had been obtained from the Pi-

Having lost the most games in the league in 1926 (17), right-hander Charlie Root (1926–1941) won the most (26) in 1927.

Kiki Cuyler (1928–1935), who won three straight stolen-base titles for the Cubs in 1928–1930.

The hard-throwing and hard-living Pat Malone (1928–1934).

Rogers Hornsby (1929–1932). He batted .380 in 1929, doing, as McCarthy said, "his share."

Hack Wilson (*left*) and Hornsby.

Malone roomed together and often went on spectacular benders. When McCarthy was asked why he allowed these two notorious elbow benders to room together, Joe's logic was impeccable: "This way," he said, "when I had to look for them I only had to find one of them, because they were always together." In his rookie year Malone was 18–13, backed up by John ("Sheriff") Blake's 17–11 and Bush's 15–6, with Root slumping to 14–18.

Cub fans, who had again thronged to Wrigley Field (with 1,143,740 ticket buyers, the Cubs were again by a wide margin the attendance leaders), were now primed for a winner. In 1929 their heroes did not disappoint them.

Veeck felt the club was one player short of going all the way and, with Wrigley's go-ahead, set out to secure him. Veeck coveted no ordinary player but simply the greatest hitter in National League history, the thirty-two-year-old seven-time batting champion, Rogers Hornsby.

Two qualities dominate discussion of Rogers Hornsby: his uncanny way with a baseball bat (.358 lifetime average, .424 personal high) and his prickly personality. Rogers had spent his first eleven big-league seasons with the Cardinals, hitting and managing them to their first pennant and world championship in 1926. But after speaking too bluntly to owner Sam Breadon, Hornsby was traded to the Gi-

Left to right: Joe McCarthy, Kenesaw Mountain Landis, and Philadelphia
A's manager Connie Mack at the 1929 World Series.

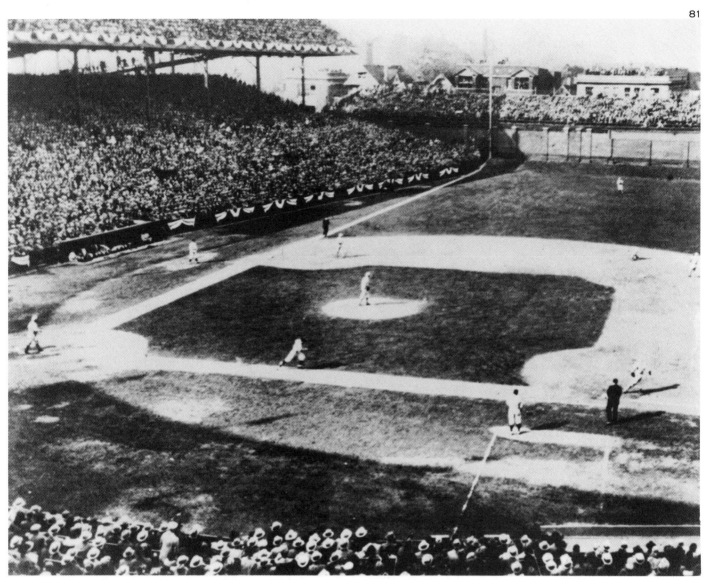

A bit of action from the 1929 World Series. The Cubs' Norm McMillan has just grounded to the A's Joe Boley at shortstop in the bottom of the first inning of Game 2. Notice that the ivy has not yet been planted to cover the Wrigley Field walls.

ants in a move that shocked St. Louis. One year in New York was enough to fray his welcome, and Hornsby and his torrid bat were shipped to Boston, for whom he batted .387 in 1928, capturing his seventh batting title.

With Boston registering a little over 200,000 in attendance in 1928, the club was in need of cash, and so the deal sending Hornsby to Chicago evolved. On November 7, 1928, Cub fans learned they had a new second baseman. For $200,000 and five second-line players, the Cubs had acquired the prince of National League batsmen.

How did McCarthy get along with the often brutally candid "Rajah"?

"Fine, just fine," McCarthy said. "He was an outspoken man, but I never found any fault with him. He played to win, and that's all I could ask for."

Hornsby, McCarthy said, "did his share." Rogers's share was a robust .380 (highest in Cub history), which led a lineup that included Stephenson (.362), Cuyler (.360), and Wilson (.345). Hornsby's 156 runs scored led the league and set another team record, while his 229 hits are also an all-time Cub high.

The veteran lefty Art Nehf (1927–1929), who finished his career with the Cubs.

With the ball ever more lively, the league batted a collective .290, the Cubs batting .303 (the Phillies led the league with a .309 team average).

Wilson cracked 39 home runs and led with 159 runs batted in, impressive figures but paltry compared to what the round man had coming up a year later, when the entire league went on a hitting binge that rewrote the record book. Hornsby drove in 149 runs and led in slugging with a .679 mark, while matching Wilson's 39 homers. Stephenson and Cuyler also drove in more than 100 runs each. The Cub attack would have been even more for-midable had Hartnett not missed almost the entire year with a sore arm, leaving the catching to be competently handled by Zack Taylor and Mike Gonzales.

Malone led the staff with a 22–10 record, followed by Root (19–6) and Bush (18–7). Malone was the league strikeout leader with 166 and was tops in shutouts with 5, an impressive number in that hard-hitting year.

Chicago stayed near the top through the first half of the season, then took over first place and never let go, winning 98 games and finishing 10½ ahead of Pittsburgh. For the Cubs it was their sixth pennant in the modern era, their first in eleven years. Attendance shot to a new record high, 1,485,166, which would stand for forty years.

As opponents in the 1929 World Series, the Cubs drew the Philadelphia Athletics, to whom they had lost in 1910. The A's were still managed by Connie Mack. This A's team was a match for McCarthy's bruisers; they were, in fact, a match for any team, featuring such stars as catcher Mickey Cochrane, out-fielder Al Simmons, first baseman Jimmie Foxx, and pitcher Lefty Grove, four of base-ball's most prodigious talents. This quartet of icons had such gifted accomplices as outfield-ers Bing Miller and Mule Haas, third base-man Jimmy Dykes, and pitchers George Earnshaw and Rube Walberg.

The Series opened in Chicago, with the Cubs expecting to face either Grove or Earn-shaw. Instead, the wily Mack sprang a sur-prise. Instead of one of his aces, Connie sent to the mound the veteran thirty-five-year-old right-hander Howard Ehmke, upon whose ca-reer the sun had all but set. Mack had had the Cubs carefully scouted and what he heard made him reason that the slow-balling, control-pitching Ehmke might be able to up-set the timing of a hard-hitting lineup that consisted almost exclusively of right-handed hitters (the lone exception was Grimm).

Ehmke made Connie look like a tactical genius. The veteran (who was in fact washed up the next year) tantalized and frustrated the

Cub sluggers with his pinpoint off-speed deliveries, defeating them 3–1 and fanning 13, a new World Series record.

After Ehmke's victory, which negated a strong performance by Root, the A's turned loose their fireballers in Game 2. Earnshaw went the first four and two-thirds innings, then was rescued during a three-run Cub rally by Grove, who finished it out for a 9–3 Athletic victory, beating Malone.

The Series then moved to Philadelphia, where Bush whipped Earnshaw (starting with just one day's rest), 3–1. In Game 4 the Cubs looked like they were on their way to tying the Series when *it* happened—*the Inning*—the most lamented inning in Chicago Cub history, one of the most famous in World Series annals.

With Root cruising along with a smooth three-hitter, the Cubs led going into the bottom of the seventh by a comfortable 8–0 score.

"We never thought we were out of a game, no matter the score," said a nostalgic Jimmy Dykes years later about that Athletic team.

What happened in the bottom of that seventh inning needs no embellishment. Al Simmons led off with a home run, making the score 8–1. Jimmie Foxx singled. Bing Miller singled when Wilson lost his ball in the sun. Dykes singled, scoring Foxx. 8–2. Joe Boley singled, scoring Miller. 8–3. Pinch-hitter George Burns popped out. Max Bishop singled, scoring Dykes. 8–4. Left-hander Art Nehf relieved Root. Mule Haas hit a drive to center that Wilson again lost in the sun; this time the ball rolled out to deep center for an inside-the-park home run. 8–7. Mickey Cochrane walked. Sheriff Blake replaced Nehf. Simmons, starting the second go-around of the inning, singled. Foxx singled, scoring Cochrane. 8–8. Malone replaced Blake. Miller was hit by a pitch, loading the bases. Dykes doubled, scoring Simmons and Foxx. 10–8. Malone then fanned the next two men, Boley and Burns (the pinch hitter, who made two outs in the inning).

Right-hander John ("Sheriff") Blake, who pitched for the Cubs from 1924 to 1931. His best year was 17–11 in 1928.

Mack sent Lefty Grove in to protect the lead over the last two innings.

"That's some relief pitcher, eh?" McCarthy said ruefully. "Lefty Grove. He came out firing bullets, and that was that."

Stunned in Game 4, the Cubs were shocked in Game 5. McCarthy's men scored 2 runs in the top of the fourth, disposing of Game 1 nemesis Ehmke, and Malone carried a 2–0, 2-hitter into the bottom of the ninth. Whereupon the Athletics uncoiled again.

With one out, Bishop singled, and Haas

tied it with a home run. After another out, Cochrane doubled, Foxx was walked, and Miller doubled home Cochrane, giving the A's a 3–2 win and the championship.

The backbiters and second-guessers were out in full force as soon as the Series was over. The hapless Wilson got his full share of censure for having lost two balls in the sun, while McCarthy was picked at for his selection of pitchers.

Winter's rough winds swept away much of the disappointment felt by Cub fans. One of them, however, remained perturbed by the painful course the Series had taken, and he was the most important one of all. Time did not mollify the dissatisfaction felt by William Wrigley, who continued to maintain that the Cubs had lost a World Series they should have won.

When McCarthy heard about his employer's unappeasable feelings, the shrewd skipper judged the situation correctly. In a private, off-the-record conversation with a sportswriter, Joe confided that win, lose, or draw in 1930, the Cubs would have a new manager in 1931, if not sooner.

EVERY THREE YEARS

THE decade that began with economic failure spreading its dreary inertia across the land saw the National League launch the most thunderous hitting barrage in baseball history, with the liveliest of lively balls being cracked so often and so soundly that one wonders if many of the offensive records established that year should not have asterisks next to them.

In 1930 the National League as a whole batted .303, with six teams batting over .300, including an all-time high .319 average posted by the Giants, .315 by the last-place Phillies (their staff had a 6.71 ERA), and .314 by the Cardinals. Chicago's contribution to the onslaught was a .309 team average and .481 slugging average, the latter still the highest in league history. The Cubs' 171 home runs were a new league record that was not broken until 1947.

As a team, the Cubs' 1,722 hits are their most ever; they also scored the highest total of runs in their history, 998, and at the same time gave up the most, 870, meaning that the score of the average Cub game in 1930 was something like 6.4 runs to 5.6.

An ankle injury that kept Hornsby on the bench for all but forty-two games deprived Chicago fans of watching the greatest hitter in league history take his swipes at the liveliest ball in league history. Nevertheless, there were plenty of other Cubs to watch wheeling around the bases: Cuyler batted .355 and had 134 RBIs; Stephenson batted .367; Hartnett, .339 (with 37 home runs); and English, .335. But it was all fairly commonplace in a league that saw twelve men collect 200 or more hits, seventeen drive in more than 100 runs, and eleven bat more than .350.

Cliff Heathcote (1922–1930), the man who was acquired from the Cardinals between games of a doubleheader.

Hack Wilson takes a mighty cut during batting practice.

But even by the robustly inflated standards of that year, Hack Wilson was remarkable. The Chicago center fielder more than atoned for his lost fly balls of the 1929 World Series by hitting a National League record 56 home runs—33 at home, 23 away—and driving in an all-time-high 190 runs. (According to Cincinnati catcher Clyde Sukeforth, Hack did even better. "I'll tell you something that everybody doesn't know," Sukeforth said years later. "Hack hit 57 that year, except that the record book doesn't show it. He hit one in Cincinnati one day, way up in the seats, hit it so hard that it bounced right back onto the field. The umpire had a bad angle on it and ruled that it had hit the screen and bounced back. I was sitting in the Cincinnati bullpen, and of course, *we* weren't going to say anything. But Hack really hit 57 that year.") In

addition to his two glamour records, Wilson also set team marks for slugging (.723) and total bases (423).

Pat Malone took advantage of his teammates' drumbeat hitting to post a 20–9 season, followed by Root's 16–14 and Bush's 15–10. On May 28 the team was stunned to hear of the death of pitcher Hal Carlson, from a stomach hemorrhage. The thirty-eight-year-old right-hander had a 4–2 record at the time he was stricken.

The Cubs came close in the year of the big bat, finishing in second place, 2 games behind the Cardinals. As soon as the Cubs had been eliminated, McCarthy resigned. Joe had been informed, discreetly and obliquely, that should he become available, the Yankees would be interested. With this information, and with Wrigley still brooding over the 1929

Series, McCarthy handed in his papers and went to New York.

McCarthy's successor was Hornsby, who had a totally unwarranted penchant for getting managerial jobs. Outside of his first full year with the Cardinals in 1926, when he won the pennant and World Series, and a couple of decent years with the Cubs, Hornsby was never a successful manager, serving stints with the Boston Braves, St. Louis Browns, and Cincinnati Reds.

Hornsby brought the troops in third in 1931, 17 games behind St. Louis, despite Chicago's league-leading figures in runs (828) and batting (.289) and its all-time club high of 340 doubles.

The baseball had been given a tranquillity

Hal Carlson (1927–1930), who died early in the 1930 season at the age of thirty-eight.

Cincinnati catcher Clyde Sukeforth: "Hack really hit 57 that year."

injection, and batting averages came down to a more realistic level. From 56 home runs Hack Wilson dropped to 13, and his stratospheric 190 RBIs declined to 61. It was, of course, more than a sedated baseball that helped Hack level off from the kind of hitting that belongs in Greek mythology. He missed McCarthy's shrewd and understanding guidance, and he didn't get along with Hornsby. While most of the team would have signed a statement agreeing with the latter, Hack's unhappiness was reflected in more drinking, lethal for a man who already drank too much. After the season he was dealt to St. Louis, then quickly traded on to Brooklyn.

Hornsby and Grimm each batted .331 and

Rogers Hornsby.

Cuyler hit .330, with Stephenson and English at .319. Root (17) and Malone and Bush (16 each) were again the top winners.

The team was now poised to take three pennants in seven years, and two of the primary contributors to that success joined the club as rookies in 1931: shortstop Billy Jurges and second baseman Billy Herman. Another new man on the squad was tall right-hander Lon Warneke, just 2–4 in twenty games but soon to become the ace.

The year 1932 was a mixed bag for the Cubs. It began sadly, saw some great success, and was not without its controversies, one of which burns to this day.

On January 26, 1932, William Wrigley died in Phoenix, Arizona. He was seventy years old. Ownership of all the Wrigley properties, including the Cubs, passed on to William's son Philip K. Wrigley.

Phil Wrigley's first order of business as a baseball executive was to let Bill Veeck continue running the front office. With the Cubs being just one facet of the Wrigley empire, "P. K." (as he was to become familiarly known) did not constantly meddle in Cub affairs. To the public he seemed somewhat detached and aloof; nevertheless, according to one Cub front-office executive, Wrigley "followed the team avidly and knew exactly what was going on at all times."

The 1932 Cubs were in many respects a transitional team, with a new second baseman, Billy Herman, and a new shortstop, Billy Jurges. Woody English was moved from short to third base, a position which he shared more and more with another newcomer, Stan Hack. With Wilson gone, Johnny Moore took over center field. With Herman on the scene, Hornsby's active career all but came to an end, as the skipper played just nineteen games.

In spite of being a team in flux, the 1932 Cubs remarkably came through to win the pennant. The team was at or near the top throughout most of the summer. Then, on August 2, the club received a jolt.

Veeck and Hornsby had been bickering for months. Veeck's complaints about his manager were myriad. Hornsby was a deep plunger at the race track, with attendant tales of large sums bet, lost, and borrowed. Veeck was also critical of Hornsby's judgment in handling pitchers, and the skipper was never one to let criticism go unanswered, no matter whom he offended. Moreover, Hornsby had a knack for irritating his own players. Billy Herman recalled, "If you were a rookie, he wouldn't talk to you. Never say hello. You might get a grunt out of him, but that was about all. The only

Chicago broadcaster Bob Elston interviewing Billy Jurges.

time you'd hear his voice with your name in it was when you did something wrong, and then you heard it loud and clear."

So with the team in second place on August 2, Veeck finally relieved himself and his players of their headache, replacing Hornsby with first baseman Charlie Grimm. It was a popular choice.

"Most of the players were pretty happy about the change," Herman said, "especially since it was Grimm who took over. Charlie was as popular with the players as Hornsby was unpopular. Sometimes that kind of shake-up can demoralize a team, but it seemed to perk us up, and we went on to win the pennant."

Billy Herman (1931–1941), beginning his ten-year reign at second base for the Cubs.

Woody English (1927–1936), who played for Chicago in ten of his twelve years in the big leagues.

Charlie Grimm.

Elation reigns in the Chicago clubhouse after the Cubs clinched the 1932 pennant. Charlie Grimm is in the center of the picture, shaking hands with Guy Bush. The man in street clothes standing next to Bush is William Veeck.

Under Hornsby, the Cubs had been 53–44 (.546); under Grimm they played to a record of 37–20 (.649) and finished up 4 games ahead of the Pirates.

Stephenson led the team with a .324 average, followed by Herman's .314, Grimm's .307, and Moore's .305. Not a power-hitting

outfit, their top home-run hitter was Moore with 13, with Stephenson's 85 RBIs leading the team.

An interesting sidebar story was shortstop Mark Koenig. When Jurges was laid up late in the season, Koenig, a former Yankee (he was the shortstop on the famous 1927 team),

THE CHICAGO CUBS

92

Five Cub outfielders line up for the photographer in the summer of 1932. *Left to right:* Kiki Cuyler, Marvin Gudat, Frank Demaree, Riggs Stephenson, and Johnny Moore.

Lon Warneke (1930–1936, 1942–1943, 1945). Some batters ranked him just behind Dean and Hubbell among National League pitchers in the 1930s.

was called up from the minor leagues and filled in admirably, batting .353 in thirty-three games. His contribution would soon have repercussions.

The ace of the staff was now Lon Warneke. In his first full season, the angular right-hander was a sizzling 22–6, leading the league in wins and ERA (2.37). Bush was 19–11, while Malone and Root each won 15.

For the Cubs the impending World Series had an added dimension of drama, for not only were they playing the New York Yankees of Babe Ruth and Lou Gehrig, the two

Cigar in hand, Guy Bush is polishing off his lunch.

the center of it, hurling insults and having them hurled back, the kindest of which was "baboon."

Chicago dispositions were not helped by the outcome of the first two games, played in New York. The Yankees pounded Bush and his successors, 12–6. In Game 2 New York beat Warneke, 5–2.

Game 3, played in Wrigley Field on October 1, 1932, will be vividly recalled as long

most noted sluggers in baseball, but these Yankees were managed by Chicago's own recent field boss, Joe McCarthy. If Joe felt he had a score to settle with his former employers, then settled it was, with thunder and dispatch. But first there was some controversy and the booming theatrics of Babe Ruth.

The controversy started when the Cubs decided to vote Koenig just a half share of their Series loot, despite Mark's stellar contributions over the season's final weeks. This was, of course, Chicago's business and no one else's. But because Koenig was a popular exteammate, the Yanks, led by Ruth, felt this was an unforgivable act of parsimony and said so. Loudly.

What began with catcalls of "cheapskates" built quickly to some truly venomous and vituperative bench-jockeying (a lost art today, and not one that is mourned). Ruth was at

Jakie May (1931–1932). The veteran left-hander finished up his career with the Cubs in 1932.

Mark Koenig (1932–1933), over whose World Series share the Cubs and Yankees feuded during the 1932 Series.

as baseball is remembered. It began with both benches in full vocal thunder, abetted by some 49,986 roaring Cub fans (the attendance was swollen by the installation of temporary bleachers). Root started for Chicago and was rocked by a 3-run Ruth homer in the first. Going into the top of the fifth, the score was tied at 4 runs apiece. With one out Ruth came to bat, and by now the shouts coming from the Cub bench were ear splitting, and none of it complimentary to the Great Man, who answered back even as he stood at the plate, taking two called strikes.

Then Ruth made a pointing gesture, holding up two fingers, the import of which is still debated. Was he reminding the Cubs he still had one strike left? Was he telling them he was going to knock one down Root's throat (as one player claimed he heard)? Or was he pointing to the center-field bleachers, indi-

Charlie Grimm swinging and missing during the 1932 Series. The catcher is the Yankees' Bill Dickey.

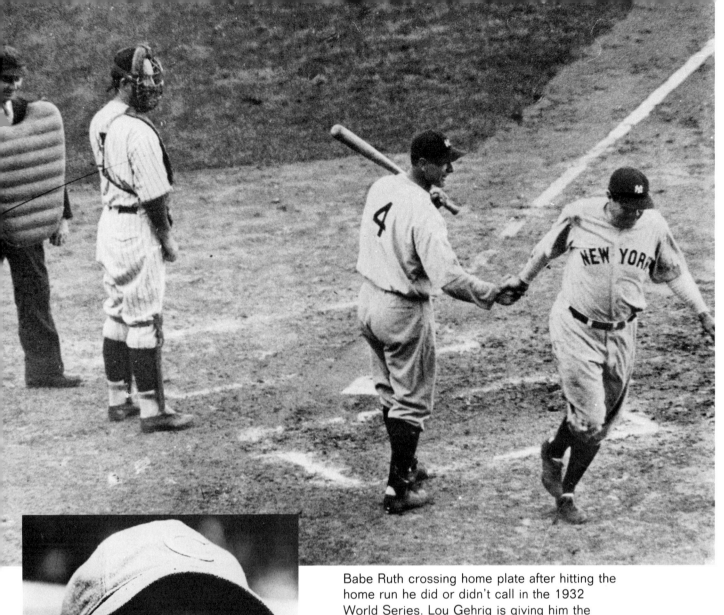

Babe Ruth crossing home plate after hitting the home run he did or didn't call in the 1932 World Series. Lou Gehrig is giving him the glad hand, while Gabby Hartnett appears stunned and umpire Roy Van Graflan is unable to suppress a smile.

Charlie Root. "The quickest way to get a good punch in the nose," Burleigh Grimes said, "is to ask Root if Ruth really called his shot."

cating the destination of the next pitch? History remains vague in its answer, but the legend is quite certain: He was calling a home run.

Whatever the mystery surrounding the gesture, there is no question about what happened to that next pitch—it went screaming out of the ballpark like no shot ever had at Wrigley Field.

Did Ruth really call his home run? There is a party-line consensus on both sides. The Cubs said no; the Yankees, yes. Charlie Root vehemently denied Ruth had done it. Ruth sometimes said he did, at other times, that he

The talented catcher Rollie Hemsley (1931–1932), whose way was blocked by Hartnett.

kees hit 160 home runs and scored 1,002 runs, while the Cubs hit 69 homers and scored 720 runs.

"We were a good team," Riggs Stephenson said. "They were a great team." Riggs was Chicago's top hitter in the Series, rapping 8 hits and batting .444.

Impressed with the Yankees' power, Veeck decided to add some wallop to his own lineup. Shortly after the Series, he concluded a deal with the Reds that brought slugger Babe Herman to Chicago. In order to obtain this col-

Johnny Moore (1928–1932, 1945), who had a lifetime batting average of .307.

didn't. He probably didn't, but it no longer matters. The tale is too delightful to discount; because it concerns Babe Ruth, the grandest of baseball's grand slammers, the man who performed so many miracles on the diamond, the feeling is, why not this one too?

In the more mundane matter of the game, the Yankees went on to a 7–5 win, the 2 homers apiece by Ruth and Gehrig outweighing single shots by Cuyler and Hartnett. The Cubs were now down three games to none, a World Series wilderness from which no voyager has ever returned.

The Yankees put the Series to rest the next day with an emphatic 13–6 victory, after the Cubs had built a 4–1 first-inning lead.

Although they are not always infallible guides, a look at the two team's season statistics might have foretold the tale. The Yan-

orful player, Veeck had to part with cash and four players, including young catcher Rollie Hemsley and center fielder Johnny Moore.

Like the other Babe, Herman has his own special place in baseball lore, most notably for getting hit on the head with a fly ball (he denied it ever happened) and for tripling into a triple play. ("What it actually was," he said, "was I doubled into a double play.") Despite his somewhat ragtag image, Herman was in truth an intelligent and highly cultured man, a devotee of grand opera, a philatelist, a champion orchid grower, and in his retirement years, a tireless world traveler.

In his heyday with the Brooklyn Dodgers, Herman had posted such eye-catching batting averages as .381 and .393. He did not approach those gaudy figures in Chicago, batting .289 and .304 in his two years there, hitting just 16 and 14 home runs.

The 1933 season saw the Cubs come in third, 6 games behind the pennant-winning Giants. Part of the problem was a broken ankle suffered in spring training by Cuyler, which sidelined him for half the season. Kiki's place was taken by Frank Demaree, who batted .272. Stephenson, as reliable as a Swiss watch, batted .329, tops on the squad. Bush led the staff with a 20–12 record, his best year; Warneke was 18–13.

William Veeck died in 1933, and his place as team president was taken over by William H. Walker, who had entered the Cub picture years before with Charles Weeghman.

A combination of a disappointing season and the deepening economic abyss that was numbing the country dropped the Cubs' attendance figure to around 590,000. In an attempt to reverse its fortunes, the club again went on the hunt for a power hitter. This time the safari came back with a man who had just rung up five astonishing years of top-shelf slugging, the Phillies' Chuck Klein.

Outfielder Babe Herman (1933–1934), who spent two of his thirteen major-league seasons with the Cubs.

It's spring training 1933 at Catalina, and Riggs Stephenson (*left*) and Babe Herman are comparing war clubs.

Klein had, in each of the last five years, collected 200 or more hits, with a high of 250 in the intoxicating 1930 season; four times he had been the home-run leader, twice the RBI leader, and in 1933 had won the Triple Crown, with a .368 average, 28 home runs, and 120 RBIs.

These achievements, however, were greatly facilitated by Baker Bowl, Klein's home park. The Phillies' field was known for its neighborly dimensions, particularly in right field

(the left-hand-hitting Klein's primary target). A large part of Chuck's handsome hammering was achieved at Baker Bowl, where his average was over .400, compared to a road mark in the .280s.

So for three players and cash estimated at around $65,000 (big money during the Depression), Klein came to Chicago, where his batting average took a precipitous plunge, along with his other statistics. The drop wasn't, however, all due to the more distant

One of the great pitchers in National League history, Burleigh Grimes pitched for the Cubs in 1932 and 1933, at the end of his nineteen-year career.

reaches of Wrigley Field; Klein suffered from charley horses in his legs that turned him black and blue and reduced his effectiveness. In 1934, he batted .301, with 20 homers and 80 RBIs.

The 1934 season was one of mixed blessings for the Cubs. Along with the Klein disappointment came an unfortunate trade. Grimm was slowing down at first base, and the Cubs had a fine replacement on hand in young Dolf Camilli, a fine-fielding power hitter. But on June 11, William Walker abruptly traded Camilli to the Phillies for first baseman

Chuck Klein (1934–1936), who had won the Triple Crown with the Phillies in 1933.

Don Hurst, whose career was nearly over. (Camilli was for years one of the league's top home-run men and in 1941, playing for Brooklyn, was the league's MVP.) The trade led to the ouster of Walker, whose stock was bought out by Phil Wrigley, who in turn started becoming more involved with the team.

The positive side of the Cubs' third-place finish in 1934 was Warneke's 22–10 record (which included back-to-back 1-hitters), Cuyler's team-leading .338 average (Kiki's last big year in Chicago), the installation of Stan

Many a rueful Cub fan began a sentence with, "If we would have kept Dolf Camilli. . . ." The future MVP (with Brooklyn) played briefly for Chicago in 1933 and 1934.

One of the Cubs' greatest batteries: Gabby Hartnett *(left)* and Lon Warneke.

Hack as regular third baseman, and the arrival of newcomers Augie Galan, Phil Cavarretta, and Bill Lee. Originally a second baseman, Galan was soon converted to an outfielder; Cavarretta, an eighteen-year-old native Chicagoan, was beginning what was to be the longest career in a Cub uniform in modern times, twenty years; while Lee (13–14) was about to blossom into the team ace.

The Cubs continued their curious every-third-year pattern of success in 1935, thanks to a spectacular September winning streak.

All summer long the National League had featured a torrid battle between the Giants and Cardinals, with the Cubs hovering in the wings. September was the month of drama for Grimm's men, but July proved to be the key to the pennant, as they tied a team record with 26 victories for the month.

The Giants had been in first place virtually the entire season when the Cardinals moved ahead of them in late August. But when September came, the Cubs suddenly broke into a dash and for three weeks never ran out of breath.

"We suddenly got hot," Billy Herman said. "I don't mean just hot—we sizzled. We took off and won twenty-one straight games. How do you explain a ball club getting that hot? I don't know. Maybe it's the power of positive

Augie Galan (1934–1941), showing the photographer how it's done.

A prince among third basemen, Stan Hack, who played his entire big-league career (1932–1947) for the Cubs. He later managed the team from 1954–1956.

thinking. All of a sudden we got the notion that we couldn't lose."

Said Phil Cavarretta, at the age of nineteen the regular first baseman, "You ever go

101

Roy Henshaw (1933, 1935–1936). A 13–5 record in 1935 was his best.

With a 100–54 record, the 1935 Cubs finished 4 games ahead of the Cardinals and were the first Cub team since 1910 to win 100. This solid unit of little bears led the league with a .288 team average, led by Hartnett's .344 (Gabby was the first Cub player to

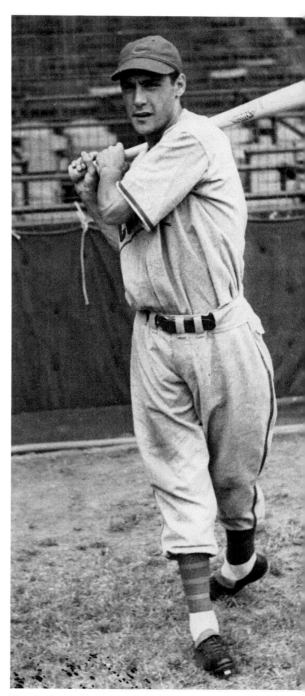

The longest Cub career in modern times belongs to Phil Cavarretta (1935–1953). He also managed the team from 1951 to 1953.

seventy-five miles an hour on the highway while everybody else is doing fifty? That's how we felt. We passed the Giants and caught up to the Cardinals right at the end of the season. With everything up for grabs, we went into St. Louis for a five-game series. All we needed was to win two of the five.''

In the first game of the showdown series with the Cardinals, Warneke nipped them 1–0, on an eighth-inning homer by young Cavarretta. The Cubs clinched the next day, when Lee defeated Dizzy Dean, 6–2.

win the baseball writers' Most Valuable Player Award), Herman's .341 (with a league-high 227 hits and team-record 57 doubles), Demaree's .325, Galan's .314, and Hack's .311. Galan led the league with 22 stolen bases and 133 runs and set a record by not grounding into a single double play all year (in 154 games). The snappy middle infielders, Jurges and Herman, each led all league shortstops and second basemen in assists, putouts, double plays, and fielding percentage.

The pitching was keyed by Lee (20–6), Warneke (20–13), Larry French (17–10), and Root (15–8). French, a canny left-hander, had been obtained from Pittsburgh the preceding November along with Freddie Lindstrom in exchange for Babe Herman and right-handers Guy Bush and Jim Weaver. Larry was to give the team its steadiest left-handed pitching since the days of Hippo Vaughn.

As they had in 1907 and 1908, the Cubs played the Detroit Tigers in the World Series, but unlike those two victorious contests the Cubs came up short this time, four games to two.

Catcher-manager Mickey Cochrane's Tigers featured some genuine busters in Hank Greenberg, Charlie Gehringer, and Goose Goslin, along with Cochrane himself. They also had strong pitching in righties Schoolboy Rowe, Tommy Bridges, Eldon Auker, and Alvin Crowder.

Warneke handled the Tigers easily in the opener in Detroit, 3–0, delivering a 4-hitter. The Tigers evened it up the next day with an 8–3 victory, chasing Root with 4 runs in the first inning.

Game 3, in Chicago, went to the Tigers, 6–5 in eleven innings, after the Cubs had tied it with a 2-run rally in the bottom of the ninth with Lee starting and French losing in relief. The Tigers took a big three games to one edge in Game 4 by nipping right-hander Tex Carleton, 2–1. Warneke, with help from Lee, kept the Cubs alive with a 3–1 win in Game 5, with Klein's 2-run homer the big blow.

Game 6, in Detroit, was a seesaw thriller,

with each team pecking at each other for a 3–3 tie after eight. In the top of the ninth, Hack led off with a triple, but the Cubs were unable to bring him in.

"That was the most frustrating thing," Grimm said years later. "For years, whenever I came into the Detroit ballpark, I'd look at third base and could still see Hack standing there."

Chicago's inability to bring their man home proved costly. With starter French still

Billy Herman, one of the great players in Cub history.

The Cubs' steady shortstop, Billy Jurges (1931–1938, 1946–1947).

on the mound in the bottom of the ninth, the Tigers put together a single, an infield out, and then a looping single to right by Goslin to end it, giving Detroit its first world championship.

The Cubs took dead aim at repeating in 1936; buoyed by a 15-game winning streak in June, they surged to the top and remained there until the end of July, then gave way to the eventual winners, the Giants. Grimm's team finished in a second-place tie with the Cardinals, 5 games behind.

Lee and French led the staff with 18 wins apiece, Warneke slipping to 16. Seven pitchers were tied for the lead in shutouts with 4 apiece, and four of them were Cubs—Lee, French, Warneke, and Carleton. Newcomer Curt Davis, obtained in a trade with the Phillies that saw Chuck Klein return to Philadelphia, was 11–9.

Frank Demaree led the hitters with a .350 average, while Herman hit .334 and for the second year in a row had 57 doubles.

The Cubs came close in 1937, leading the league from June 15 until being overtaken by the Giants in early September. At the end Grimm's club was in second place, 3 games out. And although the pennant was lost on the playing fields of the National League that September, the hindsight specialists claimed, with some justification, that it wasn't lost but given away almost a year before, on October 8, 1936. On that day the Cubs traded their superb pitcher Lon Warneke to the Cardinals for first baseman Ripper Collins and pitcher Roy Parmelee. It was a most unfortunate transaction for the Cubs, for not only was Warneke a steady winner, but Collins was a disappointment (he also broke his leg in August) and Parmelee contributed just a 7–8 rec-

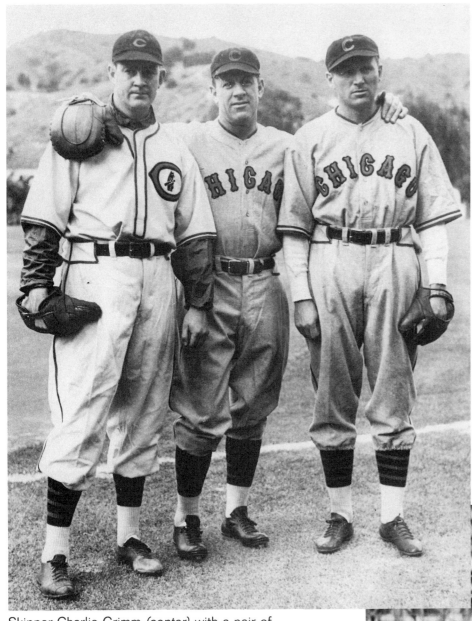

Skipper Charlie Grimm *(center)* with a pair of
recruits obtained from Pittsburgh. Larry French
(1935–1941) is on the left; Freddie Lindstrom
(1935), on the right.

Guy Bush.

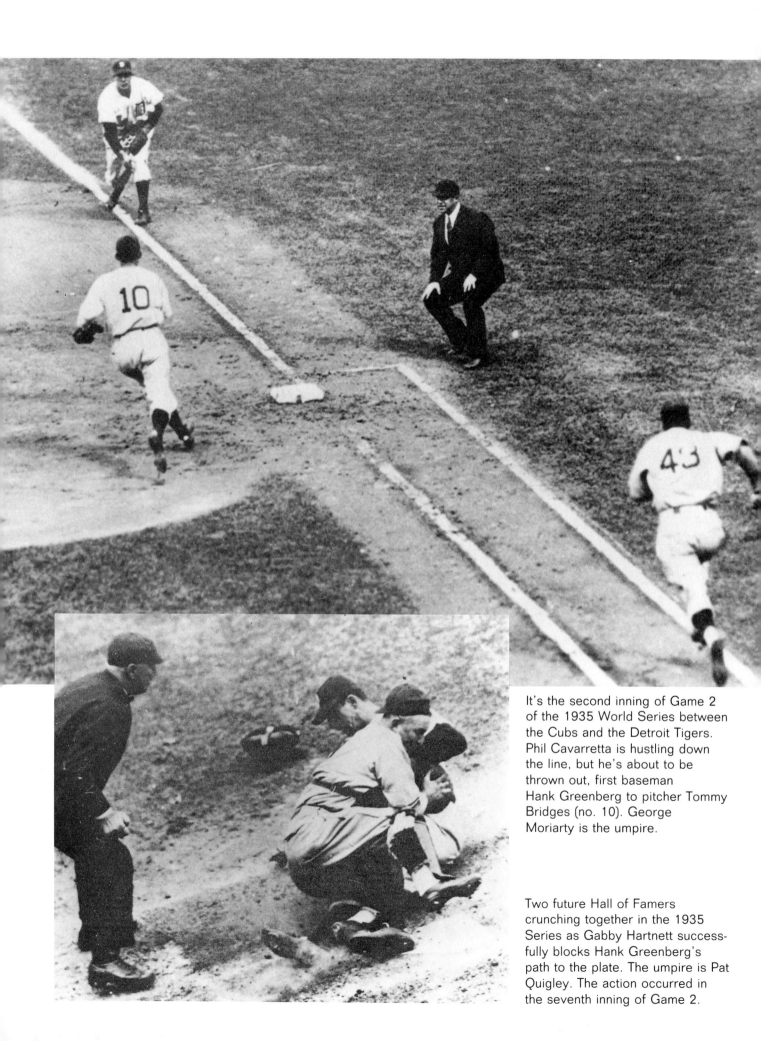

It's the second inning of Game 2 of the 1935 World Series between the Cubs and the Detroit Tigers. Phil Cavarretta is hustling down the line, but he's about to be thrown out, first baseman Hank Greenberg to pitcher Tommy Bridges (no. 10). George Moriarty is the umpire.

Two future Hall of Famers crunching together in the 1935 Series as Gabby Hartnett successfully blocks Hank Greenberg's path to the plate. The umpire is Pat Quigley. The action occurred in the seventh inning of Game 2.

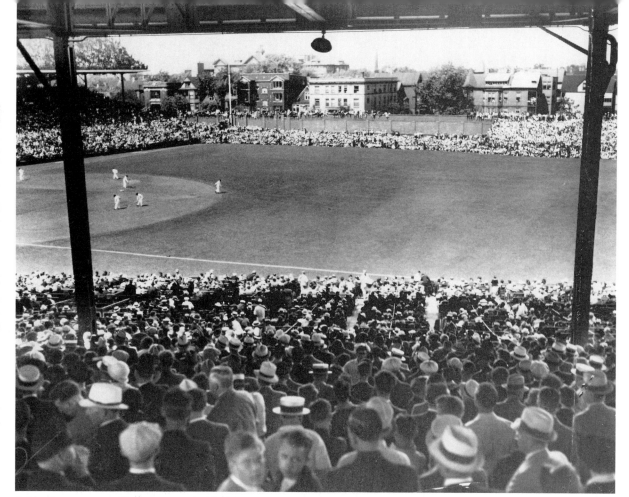

A bright summer afternoon and a full house within the friendly confines of Wrigley. The date was August 31, 1936.

ord. To highlight the mistake, Warneke went on to win 18 for the Cardinals, which led to a lot of I-told-you-so's in Chicago.

Carleton (16–8) and French (16–10) were the top winners, while Lee had an off year at 14–15. The Cubs led the league with a .287 batting average, topped by Hartnett's best year, .354, Herman's .335, and Demaree's .324. Demaree drove in 115 runs, the only Cub hitter between 1931 and 1943 to knock in more than 100 in a season.

What is probably the most radiant moment in Chicago Cubs history came in the waning days of the 1938 season, a season that Cub fans have rubbed smooth and bright with remembering.

The season started with a bit of exciting news, or what a year before would have been exciting news—the acquisition of Dizzy Dean. The Cardinals' garrulous, colorful, immensely gifted right-hander had been baseball's most celebrated player over the last few years, its

Larry French, one of the classiest left-handers in Cub history.

Frank Demaree (1932–1938),
a .350 hitter in 1936.

Right-hander Curt Davis (1936–1937).

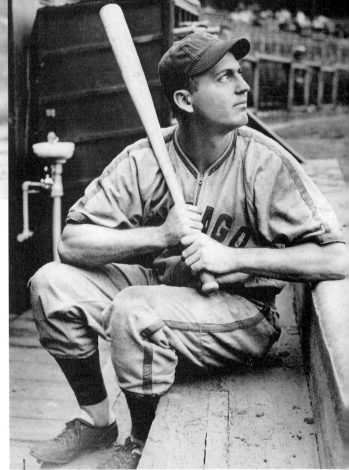

Billy Herman.

Augie Galan is heading home, but the Giants' Harry Danning has the plate effectively blocked. The play took place at New York's Polo Grounds in August 1937.

Switch-hitting first baseman Ripper Collins (1937–1938).

Right-hander Tex Carleton (1935–1938).

Gabby Hartnett.

Dizzy Dean (1938–1941). "His arm ached and his career was shot," one teammate said of him, "but he never stopped laughing."

most magnetic drawing card. Dizzy had won 30 games in 1934, 28 a year later, and 24 a year after that. He had been on his way to another summer of extravagant winning when he hurt his arm in July 1937. The famous Dizzy Dean fastball was no longer his to throw. At the age of twenty-seven, he was through.

Along with the rest of baseball, the Cubs were aware of Dean's bad arm. But so great was the aura of the man that, when the Cubs were offered the opportunity to acquire him, they did. The price was hefty: $185,000, pitchers Curt Davis and Clyde Shoun, and outfielder Tuck Stainback.

Dean did pay a few dividends. Always a crafty performer even when in possession of his blazer, he got by—when his aching arm permitted him to pitch—with slow curves and control, thrown with the same old fluid long-

Outfielder George ("Tuck") Stainback (1934–1937).

bit edgy; at one time their lead had been so comfortable the club had gone ahead and built an addition to their press box in anticipation of the coming World Series. (Press buttons prepared for the Pittsburgh Series that never happened have since become prized by collectors.)

Hartnett gambled on Dean in the opener, despite the skipper's opinion of the one-time ace: "Just a slow ball, control, and a world of heart." Dizzy came through like a thoroughbred, nursing a 2–0 lead into the top of the ninth. When the Pirates boarded men at second and third with two out, Hartnett brought in Bill Lee, his ace. After allowing a run on a wild pitch, Lee fanned the batter, and the Cubs had a 2–1 victory, trimming the Pittsburgh edge to ½ game.

striding motion, and by season's end he had a 7–1 record, and in this memory book summer, those 7 wins were crucial.

The season was marked by a midsummer managerial change, one that invoked the same magic as the one in 1932 had. On July 20, with the team in fourth place with a 45–36 record, Grimm resigned and was replaced by Hartnett, who was still catching, albeit in fewer games. The personable Grimm, always a Wrigley favorite, soon found employment as part of the team's broadcasting crew.

With Gabby at the helm, the team perked up to a 44–27 finish, at the end catching and passing the Pirates, who had sat atop the pack through most of the season's second half.

On September 27 the Pirates invaded Wrigley Field for a three-game series, leading the Cubs by 1½ games. The Pirates were a

Charlie Grimm.

Gabby Hartnett, coming home after hitting his "Homer in the Gloamin' " against the Pirates.

The following day produced baseball drama at its purest. Tied after six at 3–3, each team scored twice in the eighth. Going into the bottom of the ninth, the score remained tied. And it was getting dark. The Pirates were three outs from a tie; for the Cubs it would be an expensive tie, for Hartnett had used six pitchers in trying to keep the Pirates at bay. A tie would have forced a doubleheader the next day, an ordeal for Gabby's exhausted staff.

Mace Brown, Pittsburgh's ace reliever, retired the first two Cubs, then flashed two strikes past the next hitter, Hartnett. Gabby tells what happened on the next pitch:

"Brown wound up and let fly; I swung with everything I had and then I got that feeling—the kind of feeling you get when the blood rushes out of your head and you get dizzy."

Gabby knew he had hit one, the big one, the biggest single blow in Cub history, the famous "Homer in the Gloamin'." The ball shot through the failing light and disappeared into the left-field bleachers.

Wrigley Field became engulfed in joyous hysteria as the fans poured onto the field. Hartnett needed a wedge of teammates to help him round the bases. The moment his spiked shoe came down on home plate, the Cubs were in first place by ½ game.

The infield of the 1938 National League pennant winners. *Left to right*: Ripper Collins, Billy Herman, Billy Jurges, and Stan Hack.

Bill Lee (1934–1943, 1947), who was unbeatable during the Cubs' stretch drive to the pennant in 1938.

Clay Bryant (1935–1940), whose promising career was aborted by arm trouble.

cago pennant winner definitely lacked a big stick: Ripper Collins's 13 homers were high and, remarkably, Augie Galan's 69 RBIs were tops on the team (fourteen other National League players drove in more runs than the top man on the pennant winners).

Cub fans with a sense of history felt an ominous sense of déjà vu as their club headed into the World Series. Their team was to meet its 1932 opponents the Yankees, who were in the midst of four consecutive world

Stan Hack.

Hartnett's electrifying home run left the Pirates thoroughly demoralized. The next day Bill Lee and his mates bulldozed the Pittsburghers by a 10–1 score. The pennant was clinched a few days later. The final margin was 2 games.

Lee was the cutting edge of the staff, putting together a 22–9 record, including a league-leading 9 shutouts, 4 of which were hurled in succession during the September pennant run. His 2.66 ERA was the league's lowest. Right-hander Clay Bryant was 19–11, leading the league with 135 strikeouts. (Bryant hurt his arm the next year and ceased being a factor on the Cub staff.) No other Cub pitcher won more than 10.

Stan Hack's .320 average headed the team, with outfielder Carl Reynolds's .302 the only other mark over .300 on the squad. This Chi-

Opposing managers Gabby Hartnett *(left)* and the Yankees'
Joe McCarthy, meeting at the 1938 World Series.

Gathering at the 1938 World Series are *(left to right):* Ripper Collins, the Yankee's George Selkirk, and Ken O'Dea (1935–1938), backup catcher for the Cubs. The idea behind the photo was the "Rochester connection." Collins had played in the city in upstate New York, Selkirk lived there, and O'Dea hailed from nearby Lima.

championships and who were still managed by Joe McCarthy. Once more the Yankee cannon power was far superior to Chicago's. In 1938 the Bombers hit 174 home runs and scored 966 runs; the Cubs, 65 homers and 713 runs. Whereas Ripper Collins led the Cubs with 13 home runs, the Yankees had five men with more than 20, and whereas Galan's 69 RBIs led the Cubs, the Yankees had six men with 80 or more.

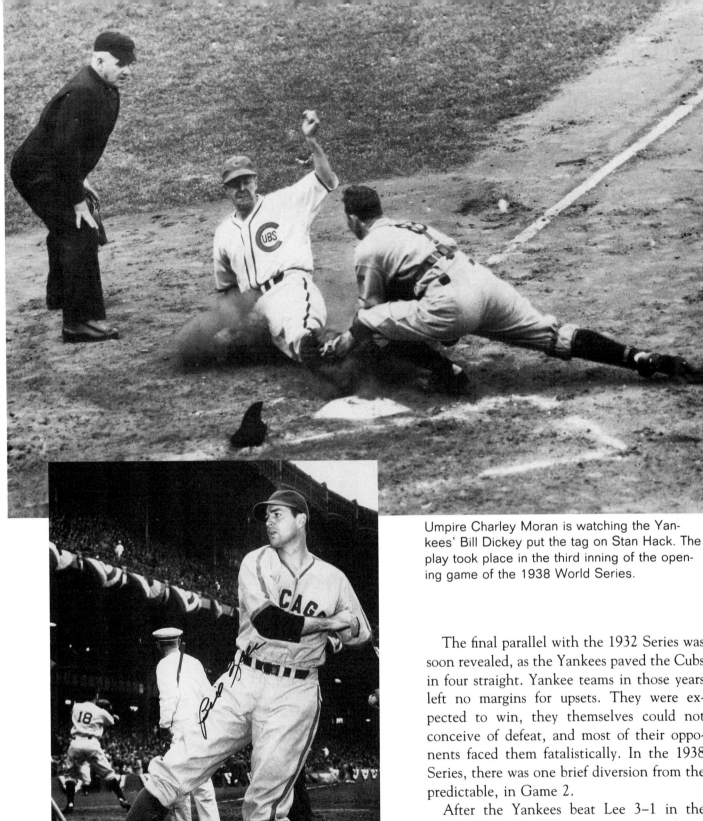

Umpire Charley Moran is watching the Yankees' Bill Dickey put the tag on Stan Hack. The play took place in the third inning of the opening game of the 1938 World Series.

The final parallel with the 1932 Series was soon revealed, as the Yankees paved the Cubs in four straight. Yankee teams in those years left no margins for upsets. They were expected to win, they themselves could not conceive of defeat, and most of their opponents faced them fatalistically. In the 1938 Series, there was one brief diversion from the predictable, in Game 2.

After the Yankees beat Lee 3–1 in the opener at Wrigley, Hartnett once more played his Dean hunch, and once more Dizzy came through handsomely, for seven innings. Keeping the Yankee sluggers (including Joe Di-

Bill Lee warming up at Yankee Stadium for his start in Game 4 of the 1938 Series.

Three Cubs carried smoking bats during the Series. Hack had 8 hits in the four games for a .471 average, Cavarretta had 6 hits (.462), and outfielder Joe Marty also had 6 (.500), driving in 5 of the 9 runs scored by Chicago. The rest of the lineup batted just .138.

The unceremonious burial of the Cubs in

Joe Marty (1937–1939), who batted .500 for the Cubs in the 1938 Series.

Maggio, Lou Gehrig, and Bill Dickey) off stride with his tantalizing, carefully spotted slow curves, Dean carried a 3–2 lead into the top of the eighth. At this point, Yankee shortstop Frankie Crosetti, the softest touch in the New York lineup, hit a 2-run homer into the left-field bleachers. DiMaggio did the same in the ninth, and the Yankees won, 6–3.

In losing his gallantly pitched game, Dean achieved a measure of twilight glory for his radiant career. It was the final time that this shrewd, ebullient, richly talented bumpkin commanded center stage on a baseball diamond. For sentimentalists it had been bittersweet; for realists, stark.

The remaining two games were models of Yankee efficiency: Game 3 was a 5–2 victory over Bryant, and then McCarthy wrapped up his second straight sweep of his old team with an 8–3 finale, defeating Lee.

Shortstop Dick Bartell (1939), who played with the Cubs for one season in his eighteen-year major-league career.

Hank Leiber (1939–1941), swinging in a game in which he hit
3 home runs against the Cardinals at Wrigley Field, July 4, 1939.

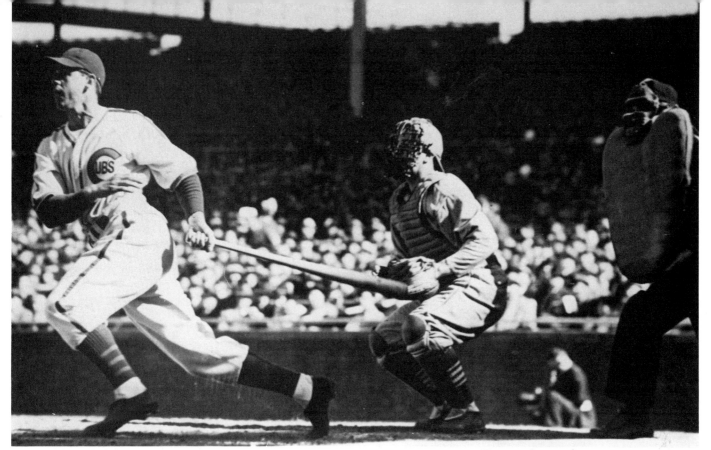

Joe Marty tying into one. The catcher is the Cardinals' Mickey Owen; the umpire, Beans Reardon.

Right-hander Jack Russell (1938–1939), a veteran American Leaguer who was a bullpen asset for the Cubs.

the Series left the front office disgruntled, and their displeasure was soon translated into action, as the team underwent an overhaul unusual for a pennant winner.

On December 6, 1938, the Cubs sent to the New York Giants Billy Jurges, Frank Demaree, and catcher Ken O'Dea in exchange for shortstop Dick Bartell, outfielder Hank Leiber, and catcher Gus Mancuso. Whereas O'Dea-Mancuso and Demaree-Leiber canceled each other out, the Cubs suffered in the Jurges-Bartell swap, Billy being the better fielder as well as a proven (and popular) ingredient of a winning chemistry.

Early in the 1939 season, the Cubs and Phillies completed a transaction that brought right-hander Claude Passeau to Chicago in exchange for Joe Marty and pitchers Ray Harrell and Kirby Higbe. Marty and Harrell faded quickly, but Higbe went on to become a star pitcher for the Phillies and later the Dodgers. Possessor of a fastball of first-magnitude quality, Higbe had pitched a handful of innings

Augie Galan hit .304 for the Cubs in 1939.

his left-handed power, would soon become one of the league's feared sluggers and a fan favorite for many years.

Bill Lee was 19–15, French 15–8, and Passeau 13–9. Receding farther and farther into the twilight, Dean was just 6–4.

This refurbished Cub team finished fourth in 1939, 13 games out of first place. Dedicated numerologists among their fans were not surprised; according to them, after winning in 1929, 1932, 1935, and 1938, the club wasn't due again until 1941.

Right-hander Vance Page (1938–1941), who was used mostly in relief.

for the Cubs in several brief trials. Cub fans never second-guessed the deal, however, for Passeau soon became one of the mainstays of the staff.

At first base, the Cubs replaced one Rip with another—Collins was gone and Russell was in. With Cavarretta out most of the year with a broken leg, the new Rip had sole possession of the bag, batting .273. Holdover Augie Galan was in the outfield with Leiber and newcomer Jim Gleeson. Russell, Bartell, Leiber, Gleeson, and Mancuso, who caught half the games, put five new faces in the lineup. Late in the season, the Cubs added Bill Nicholson to the outfield. Big Bill, with

THE LONELY PENNANT

THE Cubs would win just one pennant in the 1940s (1945) and then an entire generation of Chicago fans would gaze wistfully back as it receded into the past. It became like a last oasis on a trek that seemed to have no end. Finally, 1984 and 1989 would bring division titles, those tantalizing half pennants that brought some measure of satisfaction but ended up as merely lukewarm sips while the trek continued. The lone pennant of 1945 remained forlorn and beckoning, the gallant symbol of what was to some a lost empire.

The 1945 pennant aside, the Cubs' long dive into mediocrity began in 1940, when the team ended a stretch of fourteen straight first-division finishes (in the top four of the eight-team league) by playing under .500 for the first time since 1925 and ending up in fifth place. Fan attendance sank with the team, with 534,878 paying customers the lowest turnstile spin since 1921.

Bill Nicholson began winning the hearts of Chicago fans with 25 home runs and 98 runs batted in. Jim Gleeson and Hank Leiber each batted over .300, as did Stan Hack. Hack, the league hit leader in 1940 with 191, was by now established as one of the game's finest and most consistent third basemen; between 1934 and 1946, one year before his retirement, he never batted lower than .282 or higher than .323.

The Cubs compounded their earlier mistake of trading Jurges by swapping Bartell (after one year) to Detroit for thirty-five-year-old Billy Rogell, who played in just a handful of

games before retiring. Bobby Mattick was the regular shortstop that year, but he was not the answer and was traded to Cincinnati along with Gleeson for Billy Myers, who also failed to distinguish himself.

Claude Passeau emerged as the ace in 1940, hanging up a 20–13 record, followed by

Philip K. Wrigley.

124

Outfielder Jim Gleeson (1939–1940) batted .313 in 1940.

that the practice would continue; more specifically, that second baseman Billy Herman would be appointed. The thirty-one-year-old Herman was not only a superb all-around player but was recognized as one of the most intelligent of players. So there was some surprise when the new manager of the Chicago Cubs was not Herman but Jimmie Wilson.

A longtime National League catcher who had worked for the Cardinals, Phillies (where he had caught and managed for five years), and Reds, Jimmie had just sent in his papers as an active player. Nicknamed "Ace," Wilson was a tough character; other clubs quickly learned not to provoke his team, as Jimmie would order his hard throwers to unleash beanballs at a moment's notice. (The Cubs and Leo Durocher's Dodgers engaged in some particularly nasty dustups in 1941 and 1942.)

French's 14–14 and a 13–9 mark from rookie lefty Vern Olsen, who would never be quite that good again.

Everyone expected Hartnett to be fired after the 1940 season, and he was, bringing to a close his nineteen-year Cub career, one of the most notable in team annals.

Since 1930, the team had chosen its managers from its playing ranks (Hornsby, Grimm, Hartnett), and there was strong speculation

Jimmie Wilson, who managed the Cubs from 1941 to 1944.

The team also appointed a new general manager, James T. Gallagher, a colorful Chicago sportswriter with many bluntly spoken opinions. Intrigued by Jimmy's printed criticisms and suggestions, Wrigley summoned him to lunch one day, challenged him to do a better job of running the club, and offered him the GM position. Jimmy accepted.

One of Gallagher's early moves, made at Wilson's behest, was not a very helpful one. The newly hired Wilson was uncomfortable with the idea of so convenient a replacement as Herman on the team. So, early in the season, after an all-night session between Gallagher and Dodger president Larry MacPhail in New York, during which, it is said, more than a few glasses were hoisted, the two executives swung a deal that deprived Chicago of its great second baseman. For $40,000 and a pair of nondescript players, Herman was gone, the Cubs were worse off, and Wilson slept better at night.

Later in the season, the Dodgers also annexed Galan and French. Augie hadn't been the same since fracturing a knee running into a wall at Shibe Park and had finally been released by the Cubs, while French was sent off on waivers. Both were to do some fine work in Brooklyn.

The Cubs hoped to attract some attention that year with outfielder Lou Novikoff, a gregarious character known as "the Mad Russian." Lou had flourished in minor-league soil as few hitters ever have, leading whatever league he was in for four straight years, never hitting under .360. The genial Novikoff, however, found National League pitching more of a puzzle, and while he did bat an even .300 in 1942—his only full season—he soon faded.

The 1941 Cubs finished sixth. Only Bill Nicholson, with 26 homers and 98 RBIs, and Stan Hack, with a league-leading 186 hits and a .317 batting average, brightened the team stats at year's end. Passeau pitched well but ended at 14–14. There was also a nostalgic farewell as the longest pitching career in Cub history came to a close. At the age of forty-

Lou Novikoff (1941–1944): sensational in the minors, adequate in the majors.

two, Charlie Root closed his active career. His 8–7 record included his 200th major-league victory, and Charlie still tops the club scroll in lifetime victories (201) as well as losses (156).

By the time the 1942 season opened, the nation was at war. In a famous "green light" letter to Commissioner Landis, President Franklin Delano Roosevelt offered his opinion that public morale in the trying days

Right-hander Jake Mooty (1940–1943), who both started and relieved for the Cubs. Arm trouble put a dent in Jake's career.

ahead would be enhanced if baseball were to continue. The game did continue, of course, at once an innocuous beacon of light and solid brick of stability through some of the most perilous times in U.S. history. Like most other areas of American life, baseball relinquished its capable manpower to the various branches of military service. As the accomplished big leaguers began going off to war, the caliber of play naturally diminished.

Not until after the 1942 season did big-league rosters begin to feel the full impact of the military draft. One of the first Cubs to leave for the duration was young first baseman Eddie Waitkus, who had broken into a few games in 1941 and was being given a crack at the regular job.

With Waitkus gone, first base was covered in 1942 by Cavarretta (who also spent a lot of time in the outfield) and an early-season acquisition from the Boston Red Sox, Jimmie Foxx. Once the greatest of right-handed power hitters, Jimmie brought with him to Chicago old glamour, depleted ability, and a ruinous thirst for whiskey. Known once as "the right-handed Babe Ruth," Foxx got into seventy games, batted .205, and hit just 3 home runs.

Bill Nicholson, whose physical ailments would allow him to play through the war years, continued to supply most of the Cub power, belting 21 homers and driving in 78 runs. The amiable Stanley Hack—one writer said that Stanley was never mad at anybody and nobody was ever mad at Stanley—batted .300, as was his custom.

Reserve outfielder Charlie Gilbert (1941–1943, 1946).

In 1943, sailor Vern Olsen (1939–1942, 1946) was doing his pitching for a service club.

Pitching for a team that finished sixth again, Passeau strong-armed himself to a 19–14 record, followed by Bill Lee's 13–13. Rookie Hi Bithorn flashed some talent while compiling a 9–14 mark. Also looking good, despite a 3–7 record, was young lefty Johnny Schmitz, but he was soon off to the navy and would have to wait until the postwar years before becoming a team ace.

In 1943 wartime travel restrictions forced the Cubs to abandon their usual spring base at Catalina Island for the less salubrious climate of French Lick, Indiana. The team raised itself a notch to fifth place that year, but hardly anyone noticed. Cub fans cheered for their first home-run champion since Hack Wilson and his big 56 in 1930; the man was Nicholson, who hit 29 one-way blasts (more

than half the team's total of 52) and also led with 128 RBIs. Big Bill was now going under the nickname "Swish," reportedly bestowed upon him by those ever-vocal fans at Brooklyn's Ebbets Field, in anticipation of Bill's mighty swipes at home plate. Nick rounded off his fine season with a .309 average.

The Cubs added rookie Eddie Stanky at second base. Destined to become one of the league's livelier wires, Eddie batted just .245 but managed to coax 92 walks out of the opposition, his specialty. The following June, the Cubs would make a mistake when they swapped Eddie to the Dodgers for southpaw Bob Chipman.

The team did have a couple of bright spots this year, in outfielder Harry ("Peanuts") Lowrey, who batted .292, spent a year in the

The slick-fielding first baseman Eddie Waitkus (1941, 1946–1948).

Jimmie Foxx (1942, 1944). He hit 534 home runs in his career, but only three of them were for the Cubs.

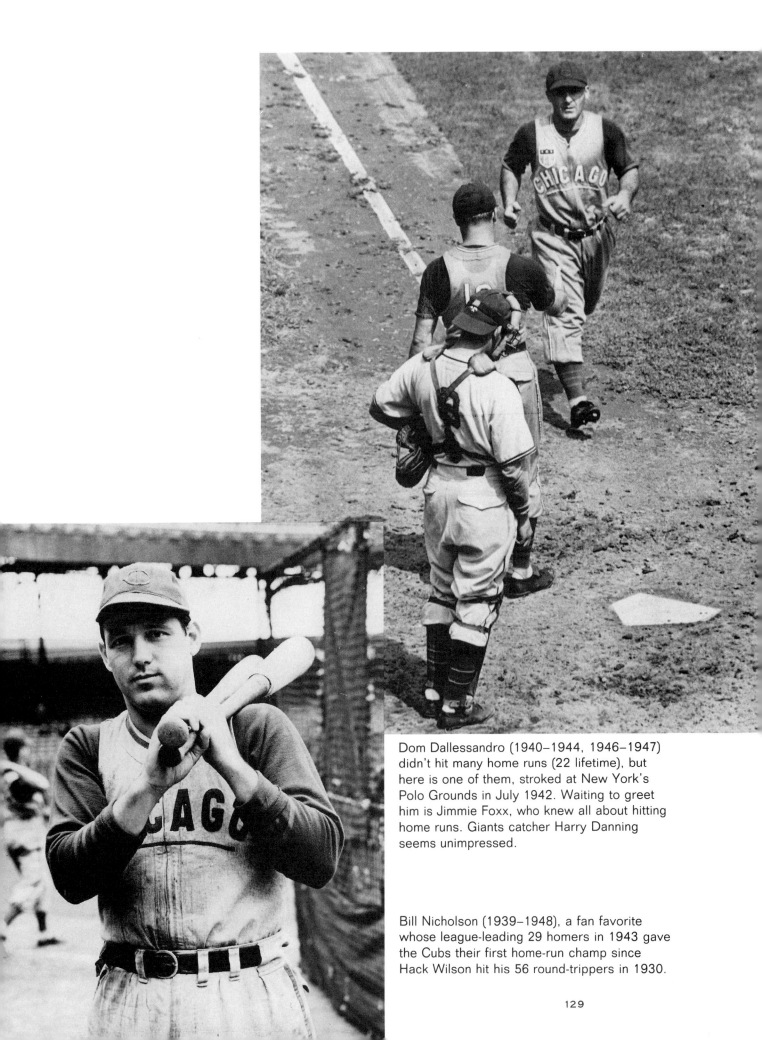

Dom Dallessandro (1940–1944, 1946–1947) didn't hit many home runs (22 lifetime), but here is one of them, stroked at New York's Polo Grounds in July 1942. Waiting to greet him is Jimmie Foxx, who knew all about hitting home runs. Giants catcher Harry Danning seems unimpressed.

Bill Nicholson (1939–1948), a fan favorite whose league-leading 29 homers in 1943 gave the Cubs their first home-run champ since Hack Wilson hit his 56 round-trippers in 1930.

130

Eddie Stanky (1943–1944). It was of Stanky that Branch Rickey said, "He can't hit, run, or throw; he only has the talent to beat you."

service, and then returned in 1945, and in young outfielder Andy Pafko, who in time would become one of the most popular Cubs ever. Andy came up at the tail end of the season and broke into thirteen games, batting .379.

Bithorn, a Puerto Rican who became that island's first big-league baseball hero, had a year of fulfilled promise with an 18–12 record and a league-high 7 shutouts. Passeau was 15–

12, and the veteran Paul Derringer, obtained from the Reds for cash, was 10–14.

The military continued making inroads upon the Cubs roster: strong-armed catcher Clyde McCullough left in midseason and was followed at the conclusion of the schedule by

Hi Bithorn (1942–1943, 1946), who gave the Cubs one big year.

Lou Novikoff *(left)* and Lou Stringer (1941–1942, 1946).

Bithorn (who never recovered his form after the war), while infielders Lou Stringer and Bobby Sturgeon were called up before the 1943 season started.

With the close of the 1943 season came calls for a managerial change at Wrigley Field. Phil Wrigley and Jimmy Gallagher thought it over and decided to stick with Wilson, assuming things would get better. Baseball is an industry in which hope is often at its most radiant amid the icy swirls of winter; while springtime, when the rest of humanity is launching its rosiest dreams, can be when many of baseball's dearest hopes begin to crumble.

The Cubs won their opening day game in 1944 and then began losing. The losing streak reached 13 in a row, setting a new club record (it was tied in 1982 and again in 1985). Along the way the Cubs lost their manager: Wilson resigned after loss number nine. Jimmie's replacement was a familiar face, Charlie

Part-time outfielder Ival Goodman (1943–1944), who stroked a .320 average in 1943.

A chilly day and a sparse crowd at Wrigley Field in the mid-1940s. Note that the walls are now covered with ivy, which was planted in the 1930s by Bill Veeck, Jr., son of the former Cub executive.

Phil Cavarretta, 1945's National League batting champion and the Cubs' first since 1912.

RBIs in successive seasons, with 33 homers and 122 RBIs. On July 22–23 Swish tied a record by hitting 4 homers in four consecutive at-bats. The slugger's fine season just missed earning him the MVP Award, which went to shortstop Marty Marion of the pennant-winning Cardinals by a hairline 190–189 vote.

Topping the pitchers in 1944 were curveballer Hank Wyse (16–15) and Passeau (15–9).

Going into the 1945 season, the St. Louis Cardinals were everyone's overwhelming favorites to win a fourth straight pennant. Thanks to a well-stocked farm system and the rejection from military service of some key players, the Cardinals had been able to maintain strong lineups despite the loss of many

Grimm. The former first baseman and skipper was managing at Milwaukee (then in the American Association), whose president was the late William Veeck's son, Bill.

It was a sorry start for the season and for Grimm's second tenure as lineup maker, but the personable Charlie soon made the best of both. He brought the Cubs in fourth, nudging them back into the first division after a four-year absence. Attendance jumped to 640,110 from what had been a twenty-two year low of 508,247.

Cavarretta, gearing up for what would be his greatest season in 1945, batted .321 and outfielder Dom Dallessandro, at five feet six inches one of baseball's shortest men, batted .304. Cub fans derived the most satisfaction from watching Bill Nicholson become the first National Leaguer to lead in home runs and

Dom Dallessandro hit .304 for Chicago in 1944.

Hank Wyse (1942–1947). They called him
"Hooks" for all the curve balls he threw.

there was a league-wide shortage of good
pitching. Then, on July 27, one of baseball's
better right-handers dropped square onto the
mound at Wrigley Field. It began with a
phone call from Larry MacPhail, then running the Yankees, to Gallagher.

"I've got waivers on Borowy," Larry told a
startled Gallagher. "What will you give us for
him?"

Since 1942 twenty-nine-year-old Hank Borowy had been one of the Yankees' top pitchers, and at the time of MacPhail's phone call
had a 10–5 record. Two mysteries surrounded
this deal, and neither has ever been satisfac-
torily explained. The first was how MacPhail
was able to obtain waivers on a star pitcher.
Big-name players are often put on waiver lists,
usually to learn if other clubs have interest in
them, and then withdrawn when a claim is

top players to the draft. In 1945, however,
their best hitter, Stan Musial, had entered the
service and this, more than anything else,
brought the Cardinals back on par with the
rest of the league.

The Cubs started off modestly in 1945,
hovering around fourth place for the first half
of the schedule. A spurt of victories sent them
into first place on July 8, and there they remained for the rest of the season, with the
Cardinals never far behind.

Gallagher and Grimm felt they were one
quality pitcher short of making a serious drive
for the pennant, but in the summer of 1945,

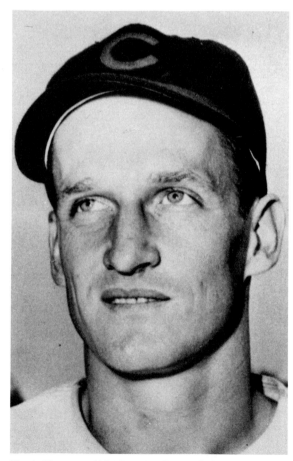

Hank Borowy (1945–1948): a gift from the
Yankees.

Whatever the reasons behind the deal, the Cubs suddenly had, for $100,000, the quality pitcher they needed. Borowy was superb for the Cubs, posting an 11–2 record and 2.13 ERA for less than half a season's work.

Borowy joined a good starting Chicago staff. Hank Wyse was the ace with a 22–10 record, followed by Passeau (17–9), Derringer (16–11), and southpaw Ray Prim (13–8). By wartime standards the Cubs had a solid rotation.

Phil Cavarretta led the team and the league with a .355 average, giving the Cubs their first batting champion since Heinie Zimmerman in 1912. Stan Hack was still at third

Veteran right-hander Paul Derringer, who helped prop up the Cubs' wartime pitching staff.

made. There is no question MacPhail would have withdrawn Borowy's name from the list if another American League club had put in a claim for him, the waiver price at the time being just $7,500. It is possible that, understanding this, the other American League clubs did not bother to put in a claim for the pitcher. Once Borowy had cleared waivers, MacPhail could sell him to the National League at any mutually agreed upon price.

The second mystery was why MacPhail was willing to dispose of a top pitcher so blithely. One theory was that MacPhail felt he owed Gallagher for the Billy Herman deal in 1941, which helped the Dodgers win the pennant. Another explanation had it that MacPhail knew that Hank had a problem with blisters on his fingers that would soon curtail his effectiveness (it did, in fact, do so a year later).

Ray Prim (1943, 1945–1946). The left-hander was 13–5 in 1945.

Stan Hack in 1945, nearing the end of his career.

The Cubs made their pennant quest difficult for themselves by losing sixteen of twenty-two games to the Cardinals (in those years teams played each other eleven times home and away) but compensated by dining on Cincinnati, with twenty-one wins in twenty-two games. The Cubs also helped themselves by winning a major-league-record 20 doubleheaders (the twin bill was a regular attraction back then). The team average of .277 was the league's best, as was the staff's 2.98 ERA. Chicagoans responded enthusiastically to it all, totaling a paid attendance of 1,036,386, highest at Wrigley since 1931.

Chicago's World Series opponent was the team they had played in 1907, 1908, and 1934, the Detroit Tigers. Steve O'Neill's team had clinched the pennant on the last

Second baseman Don Johnson (1943–1948), a .302 hitter in the 1945 pennant year.

base, batting .323; second baseman Don Johnson hit .302; Andy Pafko, .298 (with 110 RBIs); and service returnee Peanuts Lowrey, .283, driving in 89 runs with an array of clutch hits. Oddly, it was an off year for Nicholson, who dropped to .243 and just 13 homers, though he drove in 88 runs. Lennie Merullo was at shortstop, while catching duties were shared by Mickey Livingston, Paul Gillespie, and Dewey Williams.

Manager Charlie Grimm (left) puzzling over which of his four-man catching corps to pencil into that day's lineup. Backstops to choose from (left to right): Mickey Livingston (1943, 1945–1947), Len Rice (1945), Paul Gillespie (1942, 1944–1945) and Dewey Williams (1944–1947).

Shortstop Lennie Merullo (1941–1947).

Reserve outfielder Ed Sauer (1943–1945). He had a modest big-league career; his brother Hank would do better.

Utility infielder Roy Hughes (1944–1945).

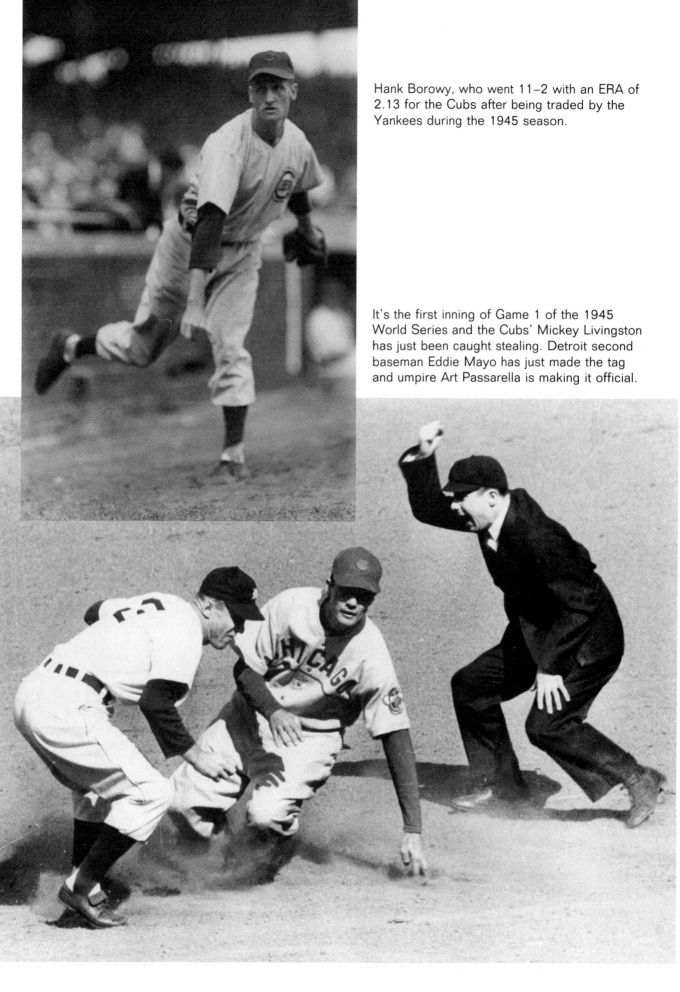

Hank Borowy, who went 11–2 with an ERA of 2.13 for the Cubs after being traded by the Yankees during the 1945 season.

It's the first inning of Game 1 of the 1945 World Series and the Cubs' Mickey Livingston has just been caught stealing. Detroit second baseman Eddie Mayo has just made the tag and umpire Art Passarella is making it official.

A Chicago celebration after the first game of the 1945 World Series. *Left to right:* Phil Cavarretta; Hank Borowy, who pitched a six-hit shutout; Andy Pafko; and Bill Nicholson.

day of the season, winning it on a ninth-inning grand slam by their big hitter, Hank Greenberg, recently returned from military service.

The Series opened in Detroit, with Borowy starting the Cubs off at a sprint with a 9–0 shutout. The Tigers evened it up the following day with a 4–1 trimming of Wyse. Still in Detroit (with wartime travel restrictions still prevailing, the first three games were in

Claude Passeau (1939–1947), who was masterful in Game 3 of the 1945 Series.

Detroit, the rest scheduled for Chicago), Claude Passeau delivered a superb 3–0 1-hitter. In surrendering just a single to Rudy York in the third inning, Passeau pitched the first 1-hitter in Series play since Ed Reulbach's against the White Sox in 1906.

The Series moved to Chicago, where the Tigers tied it at two games apiece, beating Prim, 4–1. Detroit then took the lead with an 8–4 whipping of Borowy.

Game 6 was the pulse-racer of the 1945 Series. The Cubs had a 7–3 lead going into the top of the eighth, when the Tigers put together a game-tying 4-run rally. Borowy, who had pitched five innings the day before, took over for the Cubs in the ninth and held the Tigers in place for four innings while waiting for his teammates to score. In the bottom of the twelfth, with a man on first and two out, Hack lined his fourth hit of the game to left field; the ball took an erratic hop over Greenberg's shoulder, allowing the winning run to score and tying the Series at three games apiece.

Game 7, however, was a Detroit laugher. With a gallant but tired Borowy on the mound, the Tigers broke out with 5 runs in the top of the first and from there cruised to an easy 9–3 world championship victory.

The Series proved to be a personal success for Cavarretta and Hack, each of whom rapped out 11 hits, Cavarretta for a .423 average, highest of the Series. But the Cubs had now lost seven consecutive World Series, dat-

Game 5 of the 1945 Series, at Wrigley Field. In the top of the sixth inning, Detroit's Hank Greenberg has doubled down the left-field line to score Doc Cramer. Cramer is halfway between third and home, while Greenberg can be seen stumbling as he rounds first.

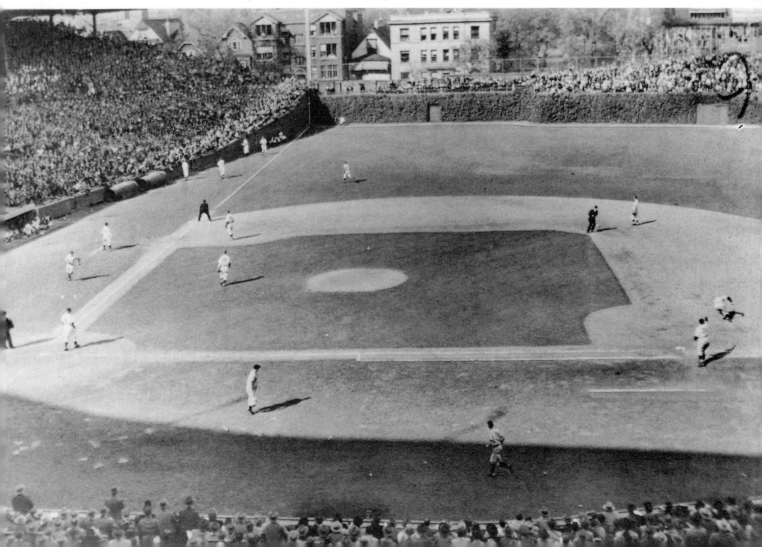

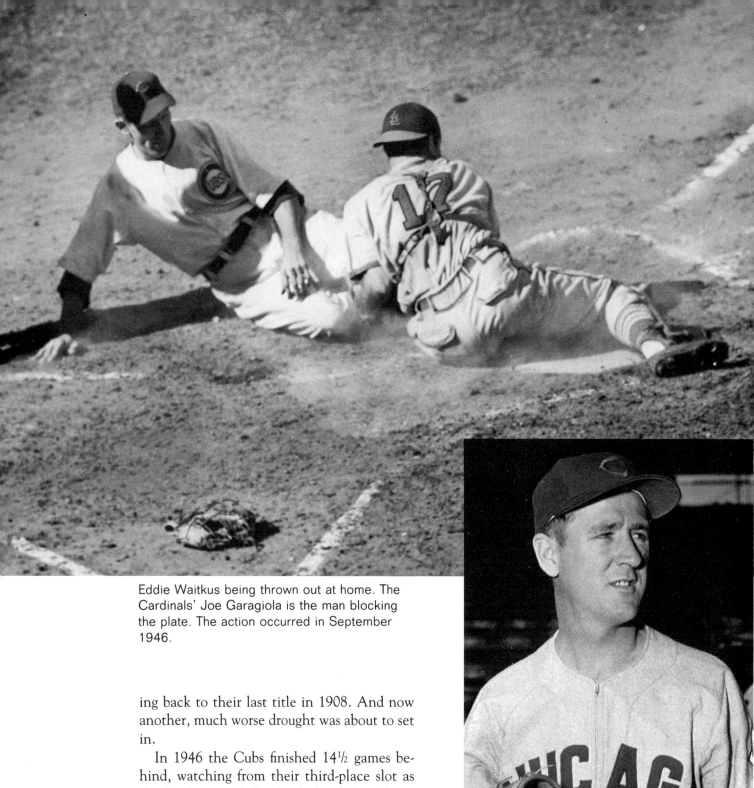

Eddie Waitkus being thrown out at home. The Cardinals' Joe Garagiola is the man blocking the plate. The action occurred in September 1946.

ing back to their last title in 1908. And now another, much worse drought was about to set in.

In 1946 the Cubs finished 14½ games behind, watching from their third-place slot as the Dodgers and Cardinals battled to baseball's first dead-heat finish (the Cardinals won the playoff). After winning the pennant, third place was no doubt a disappointment to Cub fans, but that position was soon to seem respectable, for it would be an unbelievable

Johnny Schmitz (1941–1942, 1946–1951), Chicago's ace of the postwar years.

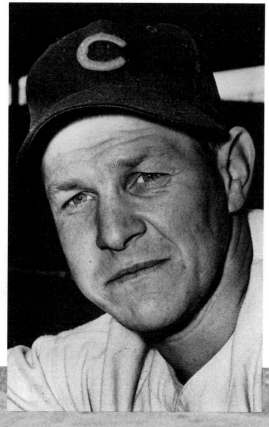

Paul Erickson (1941–1948), a big and extremely hard-throwing right-hander who both started and relieved for the Cubs.

twenty-one years before the team would finish even that high again.

Whereas most teams were strengthened by returning stars after the war, the Cubs, who had had few stars to lose, were not. The two returnees who contributed most were slick-fielding first baseman Eddie Waitkus (at .304 the club's top hitter in 1946), who moved Ca-

Lennie Merullo has just forced the Cardinals' Erv Dusak at second and is firing on to first to complete a double play. The action took place at Wrigley Field in July 1947.

varretta to the outfield, and left-hander Johnny Schmitz, who was 11–11 with a 2.61 ERA and the league strikeout leader (135). Wyse was 14–12, and Borowy, bothered by blisters on his pitching hand, was 12–10. Longtime mound strong man Passeau fell to 9–8 and was just about through.

There was an almost complete power outage at Wrigley that year, with 8 homers apiece by Cavarretta and Nicholson leading the club, the lowest total for a team leader since 1921.

The Cubs' plunge from grace began in earnest in 1947 with a sixth-place closing, 25 games from the top. The club batting average of .259 was one point from being the league's worst, though the lineup did feature a pair of .300 stickers in Cavarretta (.314) and Pafko (.302). Nicholson showed some old-time punch with 26 homers but only 75 RBIs, best on the team.

The only pitchers to win in double figures were Schmitz (13–18) and newcomer Doyle Lade (11–10). There was, however, an attendance smasher on May 18, when 46,572 paying customers established the team's all-time single-game record. The attraction was the visit of big-league baseball's first black player, Jackie Robinson of the Brooklyn Dodgers, who that year was laying the paving blocks of baseball's new era. This crowd helped bolster the team's attendance to 1,364,039, a figure that would not be bettered until 1969.

The season marked the end of Stan Hack's career as an active player, all of which (1932–47) had been spent in a Cub uniform. By now a part-timer, Hack checked out with a .271 average and .301 career mark. It was also the farewell season for Passeau (2–6), as well as for two veterans of better days who had returned to Chicago to sip the cup empty, Billy Jurges and Bill Lee.

The Cubs wrapped up the decade with a pair of last-place finishes, 27½ games out in 1948 and 36 out in 1949. Their 61 victories in 1949 marked the lowest by a Cub team since the 1901 edition had squeezed out 53. The 1948 team had a higher batting average

One of the most popular of all Cubs, Andy Pafko (1943–1951). Essentially an outfielder, he also put in some time at third base.

Chicago catcher and future manager Bob Scheffing (1941–1942, 1946–1950). He managed the Cubs from 1957 through 1959.

Manager Charlie Grimm *(right)* with a pair of his southpaws.
That's Johnny Schmitz on the left and Bob Chipman (1944–1949).

Frankie Frisch, Cubs manager from 1949 to
1951.

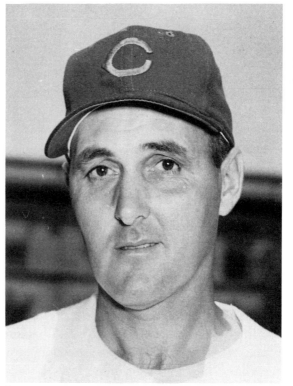

Right-handed reliever Dutch Leonard (1949–
1953).

Harry (Peanuts) Lowrey (1942–1943, 1945–1949). Lowrey's trade to Cincinnati brought Hank Sauer to the Cubs.

Leonard and Walter ("Monk") Dubiel. Dubiel did not help much, but Leonard, a thirty-nine-year-old former American Leaguer who featured a knuckleball, was to give the team some first-rate relief work over the next few years.

Another trade, made on June 15, 1949, was to provide Chicago fans with years of long-ball excitement. The Cubs sent outfielders Peanuts Lowrey and Harry Walker to Cincinnati in exchange for outfielders Frankie Baumholtz and Hank Sauer. Baumholtz gave the club some excellent stickwork for several years, but the big haul was Sauer, who was to become one of the league's top home-run hitters. In ninety-six games for the Cubs in 1949, Hank tagged 27 homers and drove in 83 runs. This gave Cub fans a bit of ventilation in their basement quarters.

(.262) than four other teams in the league and a lower ERA (4.00) than three other teams but still managed to finish in the dust bin.

Pafko had a strong year in 1948, hitting 26 homers, driving in 101 runs, and batting .312; catcher Bob Scheffing hit an even .300, and Waitkus and Lowrey were in the .290s. The pitching started and ended with Schmitz, as the slim left-hander posted an impressive 18–13 record for the tail-enders.

After fifty games and a 19–31 record in 1949, the club changed managers. Grimm was removed and made a vice-president (it beats hanging), and he was replaced by Frankie Frisch, onetime stellar second baseman for the Giants and Cardinals and a former manager at St. Louis and Pittsburgh.

The Cubs had traded Waitkus and Borowy to the Phillies for pitchers Emil ("Dutch")

Hank Sauer (1949–1955), one of the great home-run hitters in Cub history.

E·I·G·H·T

DOLDRUMS

THE history of the Chicago Cubs in the 1950s is the story of a team caught in a quagmire, of nonswimmers in deep water, of broken-boned men in a footrace, of drivers with an empty tank. The best that the team could manage to produce in that decade was three fifth-place finishes. There were a few satisfying individual achievements, but these stood out like watchtowers on an otherwise flat and desolate landscape.

The 1950 club made glacial progress, rising from eighth to seventh, burdened with the league's lowest batting average (.248) and most errors (201). Outside of the 1962–63 New York Mets, who have their own special place in the history of negative statistics, this remains the highest number of team errors in the National League since 1948. Contributing more than 25 percent of the bobbles was shortstop Roy Smalley, Sr., who had 51, though Roy did some atoning with 21 homers and 85 RBIs.

The one thing the 1950 Cubs did have was power; their 161 home runs were second highest in the league and the team's best since they parked 171 in 1930. There were twin home run guns in the outfield, Pafko hitting 36 (most by a Cub since 1930) and Sauer 32.

With the gradual decline of Johnny Schmitz, big right-hander Bob Rush, 13–20 in 1950, was emerging as the team's most reliable starter.

The 1951 Cubs had a decent spring, good enough to be just 3½ games from first place on June 1. Then came a slump that seemed to throw the front office into a panic that led to a sudden, unfortunate, and unpopular trade. The Dodgers were in town on June 15 and while there talked their hosts into this swap: Brooklyn outfielder Gene Hermanski, infielder Eddie Miksis, catcher Bruce Edwards, and left-hander Joe Hatten to the Cubs in exchange for outfielder Andy Pafko, infielder Wayne Terwilliger, catcher Rube Walker, and left-hander Johnny Schmitz. Of the four newcomers, only Miksis remained in a Cub uniform for more than a few years. The key man for Brooklyn was Pafko.

Preston Ward, who played first base for the Cubs in 1950 and part of 1953.

Shortstop Roy Smalley (1948–1953), whose son also had a successful big-league career.

Andy Pafko

Third baseman Bill Serena (1949–1954). One year in the minors, he hit 57 homers and drove in 190 runs. Life in the majors was a bit more complicated, though he did hit 17 home runs in 1950.

Bob Rush (1948–1957), a strong arm on a weak team.

Right-hander Frank Hiller (1950–1951). The ex-Yankee gave the Cubs a 12–5 year in 1950.

Wrigley Field's exterior.

Cub fans weren't the only ones dismayed by the departure of Pafko, a Wrigley Field favorite. New York Giants manager Leo Durocher had also been after "Handy Andy" and bitterly criticized Frisch for "giving away" Pafko for less than his market value, indeed, for less than the Giants were offering. (Leo's club would fight the Dodgers to the season's end and finally win the pennant on Bobby Thomson's celebrated ninth-inning playoff-game home run. Pafko, however, did help the Dodgers to a pennant in 1952.)

The Cubs continued to slump, and on July 21 baseball's patented panacea for a stumbling team was applied: Frisch was fired.

His replacement, in the fine old Cub tradition of playing managers, was Phil Cavarretta, now in his eighteenth year with the team and still giving a good game (he batted .311 as a part-time first baseman and pinch hitter that year). Sharing the bag with Phil was tall Chuck Connors, who would soon be off to Hollywood and a successful career in movies and television.

Hank Sauer remained the team's chief bombardier, hitting 30 home runs. Big Hank was paced by rookie third baseman Randy Jackson, who nailed 16 crowd pleasers and batted .275. Baumholtz led the team with a .284 average; otherwise the offense was tepid.

The four Brooklyn Dodgers who came to the Cubs in the June 15, 1951, swap involving Andy Pafko. *Left to right:* Joe Hatten, Eddie Miksis, Bruce Edwards, and Gene Hermanski.

Bob Rush (11–12) was the only starter to win in double figures, with Dutch Leonard posting a 10–6 mark in relief. At season's end the Cubs were once again last, for the third time in four years.

The 1952 Cubs were an improved band of athletes, enough to build a 38–30 record after sixty-eight games and occupy third place; but then a nine-game losing streak brought reality back to Wrigley, and the team had to settle for a break-even 77–77 record and fifth place.

What success the Cubs had that year was largely attributable to Sauer, who blasted his way to an MVP season with league-leading numbers in home runs (37) and RBIs (121).

Chuck Connors (1951), who made a bigger hit as television's "Rifleman" than he did as Chicago's first baseman.

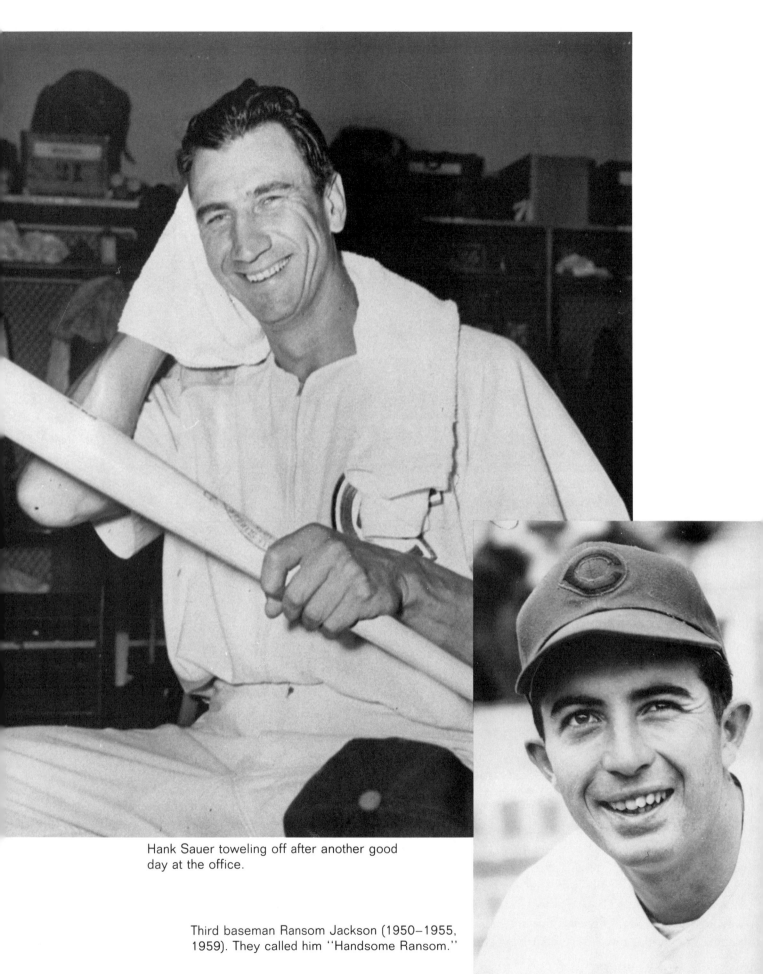

Hank Sauer toweling off after another good day at the office.

Third baseman Ransom Jackson (1950–1955, 1959). They called him ''Handsome Ransom.''

Warren Hacker *(left)* and Hank Sauer after one of the many fine games they had in 1952.

Hank followed Hartnett (1935) and Cavarretta (1945) as the team's third MVP.

The Cubs' team average of .264, up fourteen points from the year before, was second best in the league, helped by a .325 showing by Baumholtz, which placed him second to batting champion Stan Musial. First baseman Dee Fondy, in his first full season, hit an even .300.

The staff ERA of 3.58 was third best, thanks primarily to Rush, who had a mark of 2.70 to go with his 17–13 record, and to right-hander Warren Hacker, who didn't get his

Frank Baumholtz (1949–1955), a .325 hitter in 1952.

First baseman Dee Fondy (1951–1957) was a .300 hitter in 1952 and 1953.

Catcher Toby Atwell (1952–1953), who batted .290 in 1952.

first start until June 7 and from there went on to a 15–9 record, with a 2.58 ERA.

In 1953, an otherwise nondescript season in which their team blundered its way into seventh place, Cub fans had a close look at home-run history, past and future. On June 4, in a ten-player exchange with the Pirates, the Cubs obtained outfielder Ralph Kiner, who had been leading the league in four-baggers ever since he entered the league in 1946. Along with Kiner came left-hander Howie Pollett, catcher Joe Garagiola, and outfielder/first baseman George Metkovich, while to Pittsburgh went pitcher Bob Schultz, catcher Toby Atwell, first baseman Preston Ward, infielder George Freese, outfielders Gene Hermanski and Bob Addis, and a check for around $100,000.

Slugger Ralph Kiner (1953–1954).

An ailing back, which would soon bring his career to a premature end, was beginning to hamper Kiner, and while he did hit 35 home runs in 1953 (28 of them for the Cubs), it was his lowest total since 1946.

The home-run show that should have been put on by Kiner and Hank Sauer did not materialize, Sauer being sidelined for a third of the season with injuries. Jackson's 19 homers matched Hank's, while Dee Fondy led the club with a .309 average. Frank Baumholtz, who found playing center field between the heavy-legged Kiner and Sauer a challenge to his speed and stamina, swung a .306 bat. Warren Hacker, who would never be as good as he had been in 1952, worked to a 12–19 record, and tall left-hander Paul Minner was 12–15.

As for the team's future, a good chunk of it arrived on September 17, 1953, when Ernie Banks broke into the Cub lineup for the first time. Twenty-two years old, he was a shortstop who hit with power like no shortstop in history. He was to spend his entire nineteen-

Later to become a popular broadcaster, Joe Garagiola caught for the Cubs in 1953–1954.

Utility infielder Bob Ramazzotti (1949–1953).

Hank Sauer *(left)* and
Ralph Kiner. They were never
quite the home-run duo
Chicago had hoped for.

Warren Hacker (1948–1956).

Big left-hander
Paul Minner
(1950–1956).

Ernie Banks (1953–1971), Chicago's future ''Mr. Cub.'' His 2,528 games are by far the most by any player in team history.

year career in professional baseball with one team, where he eventually became known as ''Mr. Cub.'' Banks was probably the most popular player in Chicago history.

Like most other big-league teams, the Cubs were slow to sign black players (Banks and second baseman Gene Baker, who came up at the same time as Ernie, were the first), though not the slowest by far. Even though Banks's debut on September 17, 1953, was a full six

Gene Baker (1953–1957).

years after the arrival of Jackie Robinson, the Cubs were the fourth of eight National League teams to employ blacks at the major-league level.

Banks had been playing for the Kansas City Monarchs of the Negro League (the same club that had graduated Robinson into organized ball). Scouted by the Cubs, who were convinced the young man was ready for the big leagues, the Dallas-born Banks was purchased for a sum reported to be around $10,000, thus making him one of baseball's all-time bargains.

Beginning with his historic debut, Banks went on to play in 424 consecutive games, a record for a player at the start of his career.

Johnny Klippstein (1950–1954), who started and relieved for the Cubs. He pitched for seven other major-league clubs during his eighteen-year career.

Phil Cavarretta. Candor was not always the best policy.

For his ten games in 1953, Ernie batted .314 and whipped the first 2 of his 512 career home runs.

The longest playing career in modern Cub history came to an end on a note of candor during spring training of 1954. When player-manager Cavarretta told owner Wrigley that the team was doomed to another second-division finish in 1954, the owner called his thinking "defeatist" and promptly made Phil

The stong-armed Hal Jeffcoat (1948–1954), who came up as a fine defensive outfielder with a so-so bat. In 1954 he was converted to the mound, mostly as a relief pitcher, and again was so-so.

ers. The erosion in attendance was due not only to the team's weakness but also to the installation of the Milwaukee Braves, freshly arrived from Boston and playing not far north of Chicago, who were pulling in more than two million people a year.

Those Cub home runs were propelled chiefly by Sauer (41), Kiner (22), and 19 apiece from Jackson and Banks. Rush, with 13 wins, led the staff.

On November 16, 1954, the club made a good trade, sending Kiner (one year from taking his aching back into retirement) to the Cleveland Indians for right-hander Sam Jones and an estimated $60,000. Jones was a side-wheeler with a big, fast curve that buckled the knees of right-handed hitters. Sam could be wild—he ended the season leading in both strikeouts (198) and bases on balls (185). He posted a 14–20 record in 1955, the most losses in the league. Sam's finest moment of the year came on May 12, at Wrigley, when he no-hit

the first manager to be canned in spring training. Cavarretta joined the White Sox for the last two seasons of his twenty-two-year career, playing sporadically.

The new manager was a familiar face—Stan Hack. The amiable Stanley took over with words of optimism (Cavarretta's experience being fresh in mind), although he was too good a baseball man to have believed them.

Hack led his club to another seventh-place terminus, thanks primarily to a deadweight 4–21 month of June, which included a string of 11 straight losses. The team hit 159 home runs, third best in the league, which was the only diversion for the 748,143 paying custom-

Hank Sauer: 41 homers in 1954.

Sam Jones (1955–1956), whose curve was murder on right-handed hitters.

the Pirates 4–0, giving the fans an exciting ninth inning by walking the first three batters he faced and then fanning the next three. It was the first victorious no-hitter by a Cub pitcher since Jimmy Lavender's in 1915.

The 1955 Cubs were actually in third place at the All-Star break, though not really threatening, as the Dodgers were running away from everyone. A 1–12 July road trip

Ralph Kiner didn't always trot across home plate. Here he is sliding in at New York's Polo Grounds as Giants catcher Wes Westrum has trouble handling an errant throw.

Clyde McCullough (1940–1943, 1946–1948, 1953–1956), who had one of the strongest throwing arms among National League catchers.

Clyde McCullough's peg is sailing right over the head of the sliding Monte Irvin as the Giant star steals second base against the Cubs in a game in May 1955. The throw was in time, but Gene Baker dropped the ball.

punctured all pretenses, and the team began a slow elevator ride to sixth place.

Ailing and slumping, Sauer played in just seventy-nine games, hitting 12 homers and batting .211. (The following spring he was sold to the Cardinals.) The new buster on the squad was Ernie Banks, who took his first giant step toward Cooperstown with 44 home runs (a new record for big-league shortstops) and 117 RBIs. Ernie also set a record with five grand-slammers. The final one came on September 19 when, according to Ernie, he was not really trying for a home run: "You get home runs when you're not trying for them. That's the secret." The open secrets of great hitters, however, remain mysteries to those who try to emulate them. In addition to his robust hitting, Banks also lead league shortstops in fielding (.972).

The 1956 season began with 14 losses in 19 games and a ticket to the dungeon, the club's fourth finish there in nine years (after just one basement finish in the previous forty-

Ernie Banks.

Outfielder Walt Moryn (1956–1960).

seven years). Their 60 victories were fewest for a Cub team since 1901, when they won 53.

Impeded by injuries, Banks dropped to 28 home runs, while outfielder Walt Moryn, acquired from the Dodgers in a trade that saw Randy Jackson go east, hit 23. Don Hoak,

Eddie Miksis (1951–1956), who played infield and outfield for the Cubs.

in Los Angeles to the Pacific Coast League pennant.

Scheffing's 1957 team was heavy-legged (just 28 stolen bases), but had some pop (147 home runs). The injury-free Banks returned to sterling form with 43 homers, backed by first baseman Dale Long with 21. Long and outfielder Lee Walls had come to the Cubs in a trade with Pittsburgh that saw Dee Fondy and Gene Baker dispatched. Baker was replaced by Bobby Morgan, who batted .207, which contributed to the team's .244 mark, lowest in the league.

The pitching was depleted by an ill-advised trade: Sam Jones to the Cardinals as part of a ten-man deal, the main objective for Chicago being right-hander Tom Poholsky, who melted off to a 1–7 record. There were two hard-throwing youngsters at the top of the staff in Dick Drott (15–11) and Moe Dra-

who came with Moryn in the deal, took over at third. Touted as a "holler guy," Don did add some spirited noise, but when you hit .215, nobody listens.

Rush managed a 13–10 record in this season of prolonged ennui; Jones slipped to 9–14, again leading in walks (115) and whiffs (176).

At the end of the season, Hack was relieved of his thankless managerial burden, and along with him went GM Wid Matthews and Jimmy Gallagher. Matthews's duties were taken over by John Holland, while Wrigley's old favorite, Charlie Grimm, recently canned as manager at Milwaukee, returned as vice-president.

The new manager was yet another former Cub, Bob Scheffing, who had caught for the team from 1941 to 1942 and again from 1946 to 1950. The burly ex-catcher had earned the promotion by piloting the Cubs' farm team

Bob Scheffing, Cub manager from 1957 to 1959.

Ernie Banks displaying his agility at shortstop.

bowsky (13–15), each fanning 170, with Drott nailing 15 Braves in one game. Beguiled by these two young right-handers, Cub fans made "Drott and Drabowsky" sound positively lyrical. The former maestro of the mound corps, Bob Rush, sank to 6–16 and was traded to Milwaukee after the season. Reliever Turk Lown appeared 67 times, setting a new team high.

Scheffing's Cubs won two more games than the year before and popped out of the basement for a seventh-place tie with Pittsburgh.

The 1958 Cubs gave their fans plenty to cheer about—and many more came out to cheer, as attendance jumped more than 300,000, to 979,904, highest since 1952.

First baseman Dale Long (1957–1959), who did some heavy hitting for the Cubs.

165

A starter for Chicago, Moe Drabowsky (1956–1960) later was a fine reliever with the Baltimore Orioles.

(TOP LEFT) Outfielder Lee Walls (1957–1959) hit .304 in 1958.

(BOTTOM LEFT) Dick Drott (1957–1961). A sore arm curtailed what might have been an outstanding career.

Relief pitcher Omar (Turk) Lown (1951–1954, 1956–1957).

Ernie Banks.

What they were cheering were home runs—a team-record 182 of them. The leader of the band was Banks, who became the first member of a team with a losing record to be voted Most Valuable Player. Ernie did it on the strength of league-leading figures in home runs (47, breaking his own record for shortstops), RBIs (129), and slugging (.614), all of it polished up with a .313 batting average. The only blemish on Ernie's year was 32 errors, most by a shortstop.

Ernie was the bass drum in the home-run band, but he was accompanied by some pretty solid noisemakers. Including Banks, five Cubs hit 20 or more eye-poppers that year: Moryn (26), Walls (24), Bobby Thomson (21), and Long (20). Thomson, author of history's most resounding home run, had been acquired from the Giants in the spring. The team's home-run total gave them the league lead for the first time since 1930.

Bobby Thomson (1958–1959), the man who hit the "shot heard 'round the world."

Alvin Dark (1958–1959). The onetime star shortstop played third base for the Cubs late in his career.

Glen Hobbie (1957–1964), for several years the ace of the staff.

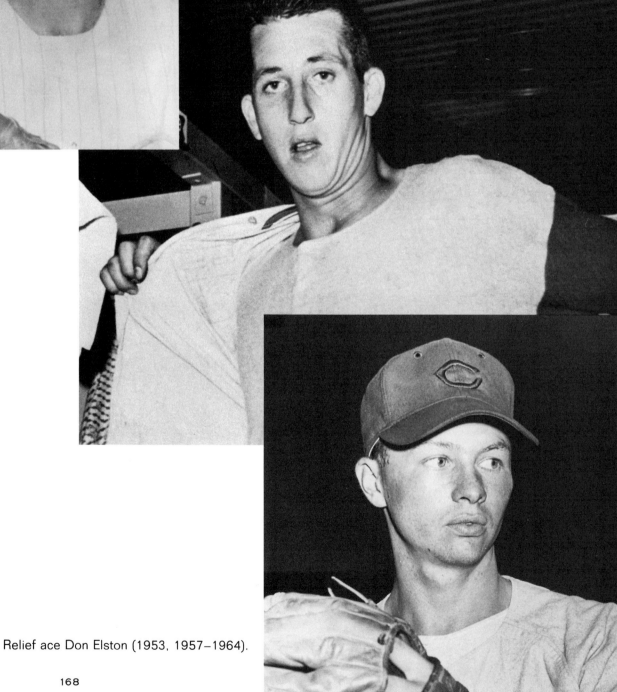

Relief ace Don Elston (1953, 1957–1964).

Jim Brosnan (1954, 1956–1958), who turned in some excellent relief work for the Cubs. He later wrote *The Long Season* and *Pennant Race*, two of the finest works in baseball literature.

In addition, the team had a flashy new second baseman in Tony Taylor, who batted only .235 but who showed promise. The veteran Alvin Dark, picked up from the Cardinals early in the season, batted .295, helping the club to a .265 average, one point under the league leader.

Despite tying for fifth place at the end with a 72–82 record, the 1958 Cubs did have their moments. As late as mid-July, they were just 2½ games from the top, albeit in fifth place. But then a dark cloud engulfed the team, and a late-July and August capsize of 23 losses in 33 games splashed cold water onto their high hopes.

Along with a somewhat sluggish defense, the problem in 1958 was a sharp decline in pitching. Neither Drott nor Drabowsky ful-

filled the expectations established in 1957, with Drott falling to 7–11 and Drabowsky, slowed by an aching elbow, to 9–11. Despite all the hitting, newcomer Glen Hobbie with a 10–6 record was the only staff member to win in double figures. With the starters completing the fewest games in the league (27), reliever Don Elston was summoned 69 times, breaking the club record set by Lown the year before.

A year later, the Cubs were still hitting home runs—163 of them. Again it was Ernie Banks in the vanguard, having what was probably his greatest all-around season. He hit 45 home runs (losing by one the league title to Eddie Mathews), batted .304, led with 143 RBIs (most in the league since 1937), and made it a complete year by setting records

A pitcher's nightmare: Ernie Banks with an armload of bats.

Ernie Banks receiving from National League president Warren Giles a plaque for having been voted the league's Most Valuable Player in 1959.

Catcher Sammy Taylor (1958–1962).

(both since broken) for shortstops with the fewest errors (12) and highest fielding average (.985). Banks, who didn't miss a game all season, became the first back-to-back MVP in National League history.

Unlike the previous year, Cub home-run hitting was scattered more widely throughout the club, with eight men (including Banks) hitting in double figures, but only Ernie banging more than 20. Moryn and Long were second, with 14 apiece. Tony Taylor picked his average up to .280. If the team occasionally seemed "Taylor-made," it was because in addition to Tony, the Cubs had Sammy Taylor catching regularly and left-hander Taylor Phillips getting into a few games.

For the second straight year, the Cubs wound up in a fifth-place tie, though this time only 13 games out of first place, and while

Celebrating a 1959 Cub victory are *(left to right)*: Earl Averill, Jr., Glen Hobbie, and Ernie Banks. Son of a Hall of Fame outfielder, Averill (1959–1960) caught and played third base for the Cubs.

this may not be an achievement worthy of huzzahs, it was the closest they had come to the top since their 1945 pennant.

With a 16–13 record, Glen Hobbie was the team's most prolific winner since Rush had 17 in 1952. But once again the staff was at the bottom in complete games, with 30, which led to 65 appearances each for relievers Don Elston and lefty Bill Henry, most in the league.

Breaking in almost unnoticed in eighteen games late in the season (and batting a mea-ger .152) was a twenty-one-year-old from Whistler, Alabama. The team liked Billy Williams's left-handed power swing. After another year of seasoning, he would be back to stay in 1961.

At the end of the season, Scheffing was summoned to Wrigley's office. The skipper was expecting a contract extension, perhaps a raise. He felt, with some justification, that he had earned both. What he received, however, was a handshake of farewell, inevitable for all managers.

SLOW ROAD TO EXCITEMENT

EXCEPT for some bursts of excitement at the end of the decade, the 1960s were as dreary for Cub fans as the recently elapsed 1950s had been. The decade featured the arrival of some of the finest playing talent in Cubs history, as well as a whirligig managerial experiment that seemed more desperate than innovative.

Wrigley's first stab at a new manager had a wistful quality about it: Charlie Grimm. Charlie stepped down from his vice-president's job, again put on the uniform—and lasted for exactly seventeen games, compiling a 6–11 record. Grimm's health was not up to the grind, and Charlie made his third term as Cub manager the shortest. As on earlier occasions, ex-manager Grimm did not go far from Wrigley Field; he did not, in fact, leave Wrigley Field. In what was, in effect, a trade with radio station WGN, Charlie went up to the booth to do color commentary and down from the booth to manage came announcer Lou Boudreau.

The onetime "Boy Wonder" player-manager of the Cleveland Indians (he had been twenty-four years old when he took the job in 1942) was one of the great shortstops in baseball history, known for his spectacular performances under pressure. After leaving Cleveland he managed the Boston Red Sox and Kansas City Athletics.

The team was flogged into a dismal seventh-place finish in 1960, and after the season Boudreau sought security by asking for a three-year contract. He may have been looking for a graceful way to return to the sanctuary of the booth; if he was, he got it, settling in for many years of broadcasting Cubs' games, watching managers come and go.

The team batting average in 1960 was .243; the last Cub team to hit any lower was the 1917 club. Banks remained the crux of the offense, leading the league with 41 home runs and driving in 117 runs. Richie Ashburn, obtained from the Phillies, topped the batters with a .291 average. Outfielder George Altman, of whom exciting things were expected, batted .266 in his sophomore year.

Charlie Grimm (*left*) welcoming his successor as Cubs manager, Lou Boudreau.

Some of Chicago's lineup punch is on display in spring training of 1960. *Left to right:* Ernie Banks, Frank Thomas, Dale Long, Walt Moryn, and Richie Ashburn.

In other trades, the power-hitting Frank Thomas, who played first, third, and outfield, had come from the Reds for Bill Henry and outfielders Lee Walls and Lou Jackson; third baseman Johnny Goryl, minor-league outfielder Lee Handley, and left-hander Ron Perranoski went to the Dodgers for infielder Don Zimmer; and on May 15 Tony Taylor and catcher Cal Neeman went to the Phillies for right-hander Don Cardwell and first baseman Ed Bouchee.

These were not the best trades the Cubs ever made. Thomas gave the lineup some added punch with 21 homers but batted just .238. When Perranoski was a minor leaguer, the canny Dodger scouts had spotted something, and the left-hander soon became one of the league's premier relievers. Zimmer

Ernie Banks.

174

when the team promoted twenty-year-old Ron Santo from the minors. The man who was to hit 337 home runs for the Cubs and set an array of fielding records for third basemen (some of which were later broken by Brooks Robinson and Mike Schmidt) broke in quietly with 9 home runs and a .251 batting average.

A player who was both hard-nosed and exuberant (his heel-clicking leaps into the air after victories would later grate on the nerves of some opponents), Santo had been signed to a professional contract right out of Seattle's Franklin High School. After just a year and a half in the minors, he joined the Cubs and made third base his personal domain until 1973. He was not only tough and aggressive but durable, playing in 154 or more games for eleven straight years.

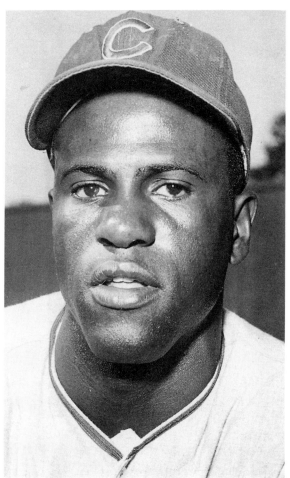

Outfielder George Altman (1959–1962, 1965–1967) led the league with 12 triples in 1961.

Frank Thomas (1960–1961, 1966). The long-baller played for seven National League teams during his career.

would, of course, help write his own chapter in Cub history after thirty years and a roadmap tour of the baseball trails.

On May 17, two days after joining the Cubs, Cardwell fired a no-hitter against the Cardinals, winning 4–0. The big right-hander was almost perfect; the only man to reach base against him was the second batter he faced, Alex Grammas, who walked.

Cardwell's blazing debut as a Cub, however, was somewhat deceiving, as he went only 8–14 for his new employers. Hobbie was again the staff leader, logging a 16–20 record but leading the league in losses; no one else won more than 10.

No one knew it at the time, but the greatest third baseman in Cub history was now in place and had been since June. That was

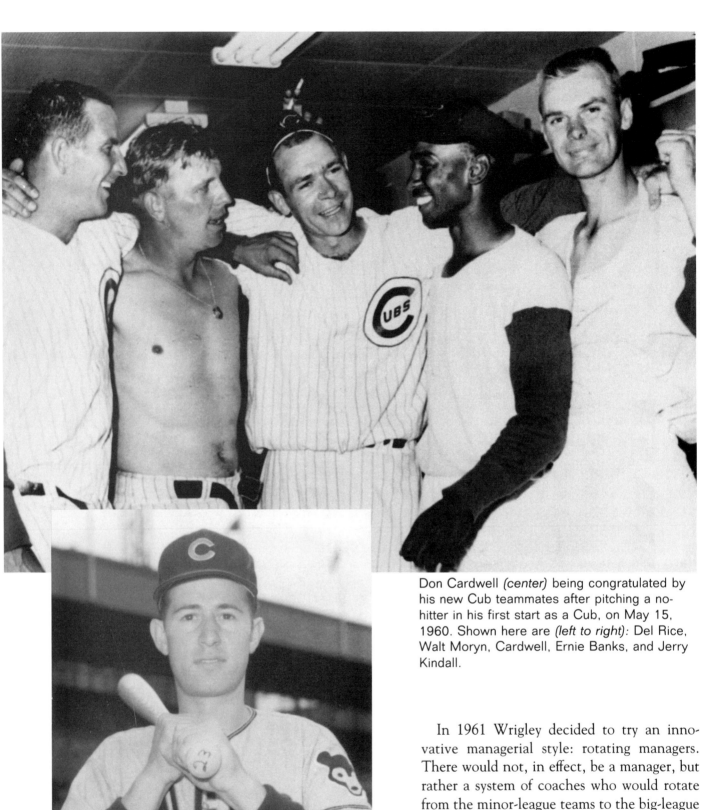

Don Cardwell *(center)* being congratulated by his new Cub teammates after pitching a no-hitter in his first start as a Cub, on May 15, 1960. Shown here are *(left to right):* Del Rice, Walt Moryn, Cardwell, Ernie Banks, and Jerry Kindall.

In 1961 Wrigley decided to try an innovative managerial style: rotating managers. There would not, in effect, be a manager, but rather a system of coaches who would rotate from the minor-league teams to the big-league dugout and back again. Wrigley wanted his senior people to have full knowledge of every player in the system and to teach them the organizational way of playing baseball. In a

Ron Santo (1960–1973).

A Cub victory in 1960 was cause for celebration, and here *(left to right)* are Glen Hobbie, Lou Boudreau, and Elvin Tappe enjoying the moment. Tappe (1954–1956, 1958, 1960, 1962), a backup catcher, was part of Phil Wrigley's revolving wheel of managers in the early 1960s.

game notorious for its conservatism and allegiance to traditions, the idea seemed positively radical and was derided. But, right or wrong, Wrigley must be given credit for attempting something different. It remains a basic tenet, however, that no matter how unorthodox your approach, you cannot succeed without talented players. And the Cubs simply did not have enough of them.

So in 1961 Vedie Himsl ran the team for thirty-one games (he was 10–21); Harry Craft for sixteen (7–9); Elvin Tappe, ninety-five (42–53); and Lou Klein, twelve (5–7). This totaled 64–90—and seventh place.

With 176 home runs, their record should have been better, but 183 errors helped sink the Cubs' ship. Knee and eye problems bothered Banks all year, holding him to 29 home runs and 80 RBIs. Santo had 23 full-circle shots and 83 RBIs, and Altman, the team leader with a .303 mark, hit 27 homers and had 96 RBIs. The surprise of the year was Billy Williams, who on the strength of 25 homers, 86 RBIs, and .278 average became the team's first Rookie of the Year. (Billy's home-run total remains a club record for rookies.) It was the beginning of a stellar career that would be notable for its high-caliber consistency, laced with achievements that included a batting title and the first $100,000

This sometimes happened early in the season at Wrigley. That's Richie Ashburn (1960–1961) charging through the snow in mid-April 1961.

contract awarded a Cub player. It culminated with election to the Hall of Fame.

With a 15–14 record, Cardwell was the team's top pitcher in 1961; southpaws Dick Ellsworth and Jack Curtis, with 10 wins each, were the only other pitchers to break into double figures.

The National League expanded to ten teams in 1962, enrolling the New York Mets and Houston Colt .45s (later Astros). The Mets, one of history's most inept teams, provided the Cubs with a cushion that year, for while the Cubs had the worst year in their history (59–103), the Mets were much worse (40–120). The boys of Wrigley finished 42½

Billy Williams (1959–1974), the National League's Rookie of the Year in 1961.

George Altman leaps into the ivy and comes down with a baseball.

Don Cardwell (1960–1962).

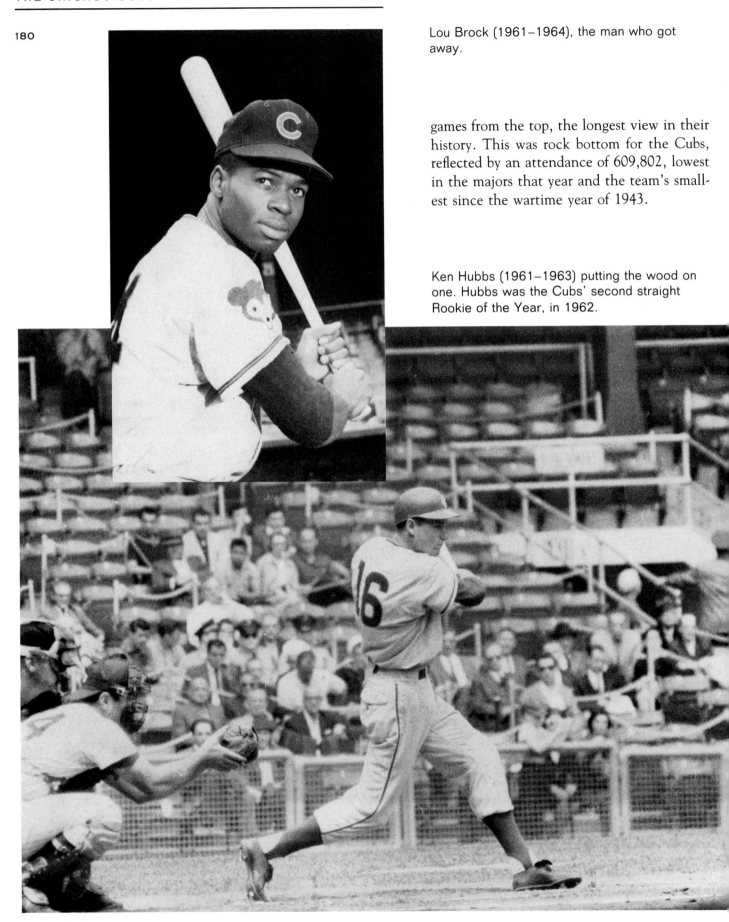

Lou Brock (1961–1964), the man who got away.

games from the top, the longest view in their history. This was rock bottom for the Cubs, reflected by an attendance of 609,802, lowest in the majors that year and the team's smallest since the wartime year of 1943.

Ken Hubbs (1961–1963) putting the wood on one. Hubbs was the Cubs' second straight Rookie of the Year, in 1962.

The "College of Coaches" management experiment was continued in 1962. This time a trio was employed, consisting of Tappe, Klein, and Charlie Metro, who had the unenviable job of running the team most of the time (112 games).

The season was not without some highlights, provided by Altman and his .318 batting average, by Banks (now a first baseman) and his 37 homers and 104 RBIs, by Williams with his 22 homers and 91 RBIs, and by rookies Lou Brock and Ken Hubbs. Brock batted .263, flashed some dazzling speed, and on June 27 became the second player ever to smash one into the center-field bleachers at the Polo Grounds (temporary home of the Mets), a ride of some 500 feet. (The first player to do it had been Joe Adcock in 1952.) Hubbs, teaming with new shortstop Andre Rodgers for a snappy DP combination, became the second

Bob Buhl (1962–1966). The veteran right-hander from the Milwaukee Braves gave the Cubs some fine years.

straight Cub to win Rookie of the Year honors. A .260 hitter, Hubbs set two major-league records for second basemen by handling 418 chances over 78 straight games without an error.

Chicago's top pitcher was veteran right-hander Bob Buhl, who had come from the Braves for Jack Curtis. Ellsworth labored to a 9–20 season and 5.09 ERA, and Cardwell dropped to 7–16. Relievers Don Elston, Bob Anderson, and Barney Schultz each worked in more than fifty games.

After the season, the Cubs swapped Altman, Cardwell, and catcher Moe Thacker to the Cardinals for catcher Jimmie Schaffer and right-handers Larry Jackson and Lindy McDaniel. Criticized initially, the trade would prove to be a good one for the Cubs.

Andre Rogers (1961–1964), who learned the rudiments of our national pastime by playing cricket in his native Bahamas.

Larry Jackson (1963–1966).

Right-hander Bob Anderson (1957–1962).

Lindy McDaniel (1963–1965), who pitched in
the big leagues for twenty-one years.

The 1963 Cubs made a remarkable recovery from their season in the crypt, improving from 59–103 to 82–80, their first season above .500 since 1946. This exhilarating improvement, however, landed them no higher than seventh in the ten-team league. (Part of the general success throughout the league was due to the anemia of the three bottom clubs, the Pirates, the Colt .45s, and Mets, who combined to lose 295 games.) This heady season was overseen by a single skipper, Bob Kennedy, who succeeded Wrigley's discarded College of Coaches.

Santo and Williams led the team with 25 homers apiece (illness caused Banks his worst year—18 homers and a .227 average), while Brock provided some basepath larceny with 24 steals, most for a Cub since Kiki Cuyler's 37 in 1930.

"Mr. Cub." An illness in 1963 held Ernie to only 18 home runs.

Bob Kennedy, Cubs manager from 1963 to 1965.

Left-hander Dick Ellsworth showed a stunning reversal of form, recovering from a 9–20 record in 1962 to 22–10 and the league's second-best ERA (2.11). Jackson was 14–18, and McDaniel provided some expert relief pitching with a 13–7 record and 22 saves.

The year 1964 began on the saddest of notes. On February 15 Ken Hubbs and a companion were killed in a plane crash near Provo, Utah. Hubbs, who had recently received his pilot's license, was flying home to Colton, California. Taking off in his Cessna 172 in what were described as unfavorable weather conditions (visibility was three miles), they crashed through the ice of Utah Lake moments after becoming airborne. The bodies were recovered two days later.

The tragic beginning seemed to foreshadow the Cubs' season. The team finished

Dick Ellsworth (1958, 1960–1966), who was a twenty-game loser in 1962 and a twenty-game winner a year later

Ken Hubbs's promising career was cut short by a plane crash on February 15, 1964.

eighth in their ten-team league, and it was little consolation that their .469 percentage, based on a 76–84 record, was the highest ever for an eighth-place club in the National League. (Their 82–80 mark and .506 percentage the year before had been the best ever for a seventh-place club. Some positive records are barely worth the trouble.)

Despite this dreary windup, Larry Jackson turned in a superb 24–11 record, leading the league in victories (the first Cub pitcher since Bill Lee in 1939 to do so) and posting the biggest win total for a Cub pitcher since Root's 26 in 1927. Buhl was 15–14, while Ellsworth dipped to 14–18.

Santo had an excellent year in 1964, hitting 30 homers, driving in 114 runs, batting a career-high .313, and tying for the league

Ron Santo, the Cubs' all-time third baseman.

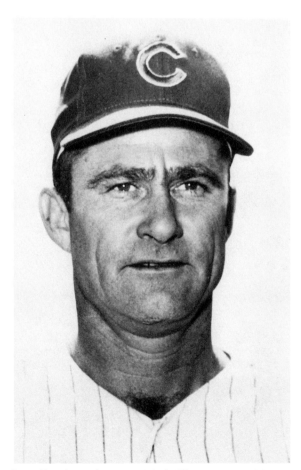

Lew Burdette (1964–1965). The onetime Milwaukee Braves ace was 9–9 for the Cubs in 1964.

lead in triples with 13. Williams, in a career-long groove, hit 33 long ones, had 98 RBIs, and batted .312.

Deciding they needed another starting pitcher, the Cubs on June 15 swung a deal with the Cardinals that would stand as a classic trading misadventure. To St. Louis went pitchers Paul Toth and Jack Spring and outfielder Lou Brock, in exchange for pitchers Ernie Broglio and Bobby Shantz, and outfielder Doug Clemens. The man the Cubs coveted was Broglio, a big right-hander who had won 18 the year before. Ernie, however, was developing a sore arm that would render him all but useless, while Brock was on the brink of superstardom.

In fairness to Chicago, the onesidedness of this deal could not have been foreseen. No one knew that Broglio would come up lame, while Brock had batted .263, .258, and was

Billy Williams and one of the smoothest swings in baseball.

Ernie Broglio (1964–1966). It seemed like a good trade at the time. The Cardinals, recipients of Lou Brock in exchange, agreed.

Ernie Banks.

hitting .251 at the time of the deal. In St. Louis he suddenly broke out in splendor, batting .348 for the Cardinals and helping them to the pennant, and from there going on to set a glittering galaxy of base-stealing records.

Seldom have three players on a team dominated an attack the way Santo, Williams, and Banks did for the Cubs in 1965. Williams had 34 homers, 108 RBIs, and a .315 average; Santo hit 33 homers, with 101 RBIs and a .285 average; and Banks banged 28, with 106 RBIs and a .265 mark. No other Cub hit more

than 6 home runs, drove in more than 34 runs, nor batted higher than .239. That latter average belonged to rookie second baseman Glenn Beckert, who would get much better; also due to improve immeasurably was another newcomer, shortstop Don Kessinger, who launched his major-league career in the leaky vessel of a .201 batting average.

The team finished eighth in 1965, with Jackson struggling to a 14–21 record and Ellsworth checking in at 14–15. Only Buhl, at 13–11, managed to finish over .500. The club

Glenn Beckert sliding safely into third. The third baseman is
the Giants' Jim Ray Hart; the umpire, Paul Taylor.

flashed a new bullpen hero that year in submarine-balling right-hander Ted Abernathy, who led the league with 31 saves, appearing in what is still the most games for a Cub pitcher, 84.

The only thing that prevented the team from going totally prostrate was the presence of the Mets and Astros; the expansion clubs finished below the Cubs and between them distributed a largesse of 209 losses throughout the league.

It was again time to unseat the manager, and on June 14 Kennedy was moved into the front office and made a vice-president. The new skipper was Lou Klein.

Symbolic of Cub futility in 1965 were a couple of gems fired against them by opposing pitchers. On August 19 Cincinnati's hard-throwing right-hander Jim Maloney pitched a ten-inning no-hitter at Wrigley Field, winning 1–0 on a tenth-inning home run by Chico Cardenas. And on September 9, the Cubs did even worse. Worse than a no-hitter? Yes. Sandy Koufax, in another 1–0 game, was absolutely immaculate, pitching a perfect game. The Dodger ace of aces was nearly matched by Chicago lefty Bob Hendley, who allowed just 1 hit, a two-out seventh-inning double by Lou Johnson, which did not figure in the scoring. The game's lone run came in

Ted Abernathy (1965–1966, 1969–1970). His 84 appearances in 1965 remain the record for a Cub pitcher.

Bob Hendley (1965–1967), who pitched the game of his life, but right in the teeth of Koufax's perfect game.

Leo Durocher. Nobody ever ignored him.

the bottom of the fifth when Johnson walked (Hendley's only walk; Johnson was the only man on either side to reach base), was sacrificed to second, stole third, and came home when catcher Chris Krug threw the ball away. So, in this, the most parsimoniously pitched game since the famous Toney-Vaughn "double no-hitter," Hendley could have pitched a no-hitter and lost.

A new manager arrived in 1966, and a highly noticeable one at that: Leo Durocher. Former skipper of the Brooklyn Dodgers and New York Giants, both of whom had won pennants under him, Leo had not managed since 1956. Durocher was many things: opin-

ionated, often abrasive, supremely self-confident, and most important, one of the sharpest men in baseball. He stepped on toes and was not reluctant to punch a nose, and there were always a few players on a Durocher-managed club who would have loved to throttle the skipper. But even the most sullen of these would have to admit that Leo knew the game. Leo's caustic, uncompromising style of running a club was beginning to become passé. Players were becoming higher paid, more independent, and less tolerant of dictatorial managers. Nevertheless, there was still some mileage left in the old tradition, and Leo would squeeze it out.

Glenn Beckert (1965–1973), Chicago's solid man at second base.

Leo's first pronouncement as skipper would be a classic promise, accurate but unfortunate. "This is definitely not an eighth-place club," he said, referring to the Cubs' 1965 resting place in one of those spirited statements new managers always make at the press conference called for the occasion. Leo was right. In 1966 the Cubs were a tenth-place club, sinking into the cellar with a 59–103 repeat of the worst year in franchise history (1962).

Last or not, outside of the pitching, the team had some solid talent. The infield of Banks, Beckert, Kessinger, and Santo was one of the league's best. Beckert jumped his av-

Don Kessinger (1964–1975), who played more games (1,618) at shortstop than any other Cub.

erage to .287; Kessinger, his, to .274. Santo batted .312, hit 30 homers, and put together the longest hitting streak in team history, 28 games.

Also on the plus side were a few good trades engineered by John Holland. Lindy McDaniel, Don Landrum, and Jim Rittwage were sent to the Giants for a couple of unknowns, catcher Randy Hundley and right-hander Bill Hands. Hands would pay dividends in a few years, while Hundley broke in solidly, hitting 19 homers and catching 149 games (a record for a rookie catcher). He was hailed as the team's best receiver since Hartnett.

Adolfo Phillips (1966–1969): talented but tempermental.

Another trade turned out to be an act of theft comparable to the Brock caper, with the Cubs on the slick end this time. On April 21, 1966, they sent the Phillies the aging right-handers Jackson and Buhl and received in return first baseman John Herrnstein (who does not figure in Cub history), outfielder Adolfo Phillips (talented but moody), and the man who was to become the team's greatest

pitcher since Three-Finger Brown, Ferguson Jenkins.

The twenty-three-year-old Canadian-born Jenkins came to Chicago ostensibly as a relief pitcher. In 1966 he appeared in sixty games, just twelve as a starter, posting a 6–8 record. The former Phillies pitching star Robin Roberts, spooning out his nineteen-year big-league career with the Cubs that season, was one of those who urged the club to make Jenkins a starter.

On the dismal side of the tenth-place finish was the pitching. Ellsworth tied a club record with 22 losses, and Hands was 8–13. A bright note was sounded by rookie left-hander Ken Holtzman, who broke in at 11–16 and attracted attention with 171 strikeouts. Also

Randy Hundley (1966–1973, 1976–1977).

drawing attention with his strikeouts was young outfielder Byron Browne, who hit 16 home runs but set an all-time club record with 143 whiffs, something he managed to do in 419 at-bats. Another negative was a trading mistake Holland made when he sent relief ace Abernathy to the Braves in May for outfielder Lee Thomas. Thomas contributed little, while Abernathy continued to pitch well.

It looked like a Leo miracle in 1967, as the Cubs jumped from near invisibility to a bristling third-place finish. But the miracle was hewn out of talent, hard work, and an air of commanding confidence on the part of the skipper that became contagious.

"Leo was all over the field," Beckert recalled of the spring camp at Scottsdale, Arizona. "He was yelling and clapping his hands and encouraging everybody. He told us we were not a last-place club, and we believed him."

The infield remained a solid unit. Banks hit 23 homers and drove in 95 runs (this after Leo had wondered aloud if Ernie, now thirty-six, wasn't "getting old"), Beckert and Kessinger snapped off double plays that reminded Wrigley Field fans of Jurges and Herman, and Santo hit 30 homers, had 107 RBIs, and batted .300. Williams continued his clockwork slugging (28 homers, 84 RBIs), and the team led in runs scored with 702. As important as the hitting was the improved defense; there was a reduction in errors from 166 to 121 (tied for lowest in the league). Hundley, with just 4 errors and a .996 fielding average, set records for catchers in 150 or more games.

Led by Jenkins, who blossomed with a 20–13 record, the pitching staff reduced its ERA from 4.33 to 3.48. Jenkins set a new team record with 236 strikeouts, a record he would continue to break for the next three years. Young southpaw Rich Nye, who would never repeat this success, was 13–10, and rookie right-hander Joe Niekro, beginning a twenty-two-year stay in the big leagues, was 10–7. Holtzman spent much of the summer in the army, but with enough weekend passes to compile a perfect 9–0 record.

Ferguson Jenkins (1966–1973, 1982–1983), the Cub's greatest pitcher since Three-Finger Brown.

As late as July 25, the Cubs were in a first-place tie with the Cardinals, but then a couple of prolonged losing stretches gradually took them out of contention. Nevertheless, the season had been a success. The club's revival did not go unnoticed or unappreciated in Chicago, as attendance jumped more than 300,000, to 977,226.

The hoped-for pennant did not materialize in 1968, but the season was not entirely disappointing. The low point came in June, when Leo's men were shut out for four straight games and forty-eight straight innings, each of which tied a major-league rec-

Don Kessinger on the prowl.

ord. The turnaround came in July, when the team put together a drive that saw them win 29 of 39 and vault from ninth place to third, which was where they took their final bows.

There were many fine individual efforts that year, beginning with Billy Williams, who turned in another of his patented seasons that seemed to have been programmed in the spring: 30 home runs, 98 RBIs, .288 batting average. Banks compensated for a .246 average with 32 homers, while Santo parked 26 big ones and drove in 98 runs. Beckert kept improving, moving up to .294.

Some people were wondering aloud if Durocher was working his players just a bit too much. Seven of his regulars played in more than 150 games, including the thirty-seven-year-old Banks. Even more egregious, Hundley caught 160 games, which is an unreasonable burden on a catcher.

Another hard (and always willing) worker in 1968 was Jenkins, who was 20–15 but

Joe Niekro (1967–1969), who began his twenty-year career with the Cubs.

The 1968 Cubs led the league in home runs (130), fewest errors (119), and fielding percentage (.981). The fans seemed satisfied, with attendance jumping to 1,043,409, the highest at Wrigley since 1950.

It was not unreasonable for Cub fans to have had the highest expectations in 1969—certainly more so than New York Met fans, whose club opened the season as 100–1 shots. Winning the pennant would now be just a little easier as well as a little trickier than it used to be, as the major leagues had adopted divisional play. The National League had enrolled expansion clubs San Diego and Montreal into the fraternity and then halved the league into two six-team East and West divisions. It would be easier to win in what amounted to a six-team league than in the

Billy Williams.

pitched even better than that, losing five games by 1–0 scores. He broke his own club record by racking up 260 strikeouts. Hands was 16–10, Niekro 14–10, and Holtzman 11–14. Right-hander Phil Regan, whom the Cubs obtained in a spring trade with the Dodgers, gave the bullpen some first-class fortification, winning 10 games and saving 25. Whatever else the Cubs may have lacked during the previous ten years or so, they were always particularly blessed in the pen, with Turk Lown, Don Elston, Bill Henry, Lindy McDaniel, Ted Abernathy, and now Regan.

Reliever Phil Regan (1968–1972).

Ken Holtzman (1965–1971, 1978–1979).

previous ten-team setup. The tricky part came in winning the postseason league championship playoffs (then a best-of-five series) against the other division winner, which determined the pennant winner.

If there was a team in the National League's Eastern Division that seemed equipped to unseat the Cardinals, winner of the two previous pennants, it was Durocher's Cubs. The Banks-Beckert-Kessinger-Santo infield, with Hundley catching, was the league's best. The outfield, however, had some question marks. Although Williams was in left field, Leo was forced to go with ex-Met Jim Hickman in right and Don Young in center. Young was a superb defensive player but light of stick. Adolfo Phillips, the previous regular in center, broke a bone in his hand in spring training, played little, and was finally dealt to Montreal. Outside of outfielder Willie Smith, the team was weak on the bench, which led Leo to play five of his regulars in more than 150 games each.

Ron Santo putting one in play.

The team had three strong starters in Jenkins, Hands, and Holtzman. The desperately needed fourth starter was obtained in late April by sending Niekro to San Diego for hard-throwing right-hander Dick Selma, who soon became a favorite of the team's famous yellow-hatted rooters in the bleachers, known as "the Bleacher Bums."

The Cubs entered the season as cofavorites with the Cardinals, and their early work did nothing to dispel the rosy forecast. They won their first four games and went on to have a 16–7 April, 16–9 May, 17–11 June, 15–14 July, and 18–11 August. This consistent winning kept Durocher's team in first place for 155 consecutive days, dating from opening day.

On August 14 the Cubs were 8½ ahead of the second-place Cardinals and 9½ in front of the Mets, whose spirited play was the surprise of the league. On August 19 Holtzman threw a 3–0 no-hitter against the Braves at Wrigley (all the scoring done on Santo's first-inning homer). Holtzman recorded no strikeouts, a rarity in a no-hitter.

The Cubs then cooled off, and by August 27 their lead had eroded to 2 games, their smallest advantage since May 9. A six-game winning streak soon rebuilt their moat around first place, and on September 5 they led by 5.

At that point the Chicago express began rolling backward while the New York streamliner came barreling ahead at full throttle. The Cubs lost three in a row to Pittsburgh, a sweep from which they never seemed to recover. They went to New York and lost two to the Mets, trimming Chicago's lead to just ½ game. Behind the remarkable pitching of

Bill Hands (1966–1972), a twenty-game winner in 1969.

The Cubs ended this most frustrating of seasons with a 92–70 record, their best showing since 1945 and a better mark than the pennant winners of 1932 and 1938 had. But the Mets had won 100, and after the New Yorkers swept Atlanta in the playoffs and whipped a vastly superior Baltimore team in the World Series, they were proclaimed "miracle" workers.

Miracles notwithstanding, however, there was some grumbling in Chicago, most pointedly about Durocher having burdened his players with excessive playing time. At the age of thirty-eight, Banks was in 155 games; Kessinger, in 158; Santo, in 160; Hundley caught 151; and Williams was in 163. (Williams had, in fact, now played in a league-record 982 consecutive games.) With all this heavy work, there were some fine performances. Banks had the last of his many productive seasons, with 23 homers and 106 RBIs; Santo hit 29 home runs and drove in 123 runs; and Williams had 21 one-way shots and 95 RBIs. The .230 bats of Young and Hickman, however, were heavy burdens.

Jenkins (21–15) and Hands (20–14) were the big winners, with each starting more than forty games and pitching more than 300 innings. Jenkins's 42 starts constituted a new team record, and once more he broke his own club mark with 273 strikeouts, leading the league. Holtzman was 17–13, slipping to a 1–5 September. The fourth starter, Selma, was 10–8. Phil Regan and a reacquired Ted Abernathy did most of the relief work.

The summer of excitement helped the Cubs set a new club attendance mark of 1,674,993. But disappointment was sharp, and the memory of it long lasting.

"Those last three weeks," Ron Santo said later, "were a nightmare."

Tom Seaver and Jerry Koosman, who between them won 19 of their last 20 decisions, the Mets had become almost unbeatable. Two more losses to the Phillies knocked the Cubs from the top, and they never made it back. The September records of the two clubs tell the whole story: Mets 23–7, Cubs 8–17. From August 13, when they were 8½ back, the Mets' record was 38–11, a difficult onslaught to offset.

T·E·N

GRADUAL DECLINE

THE feeling in many National League quarters as the 1970 season began was that miracles, like lightning, do not strike twice in the same place, and consequently the Mets were not expected to repeat as winners in the Eastern Division. Those who held this conviction were proved correct, while those who felt that this year, finally, would be Chicago's, were proved wrong. Danny Murtaugh's Pirates began what would be a decade of Pennsylvania domination of the division, as the Pirates won six times, and the Phillies, three.

There were some new faces and significant cast changes at Wrigley Field in 1970. Durocher had been saying for some time that Ernie Banks was getting along in years, and if you say that long enough about someone, you will eventually be right. Mr. Cub made a deep concession to those years Leo had been talking about and played in just seventy-two games. Appearing at first base when Ernie did not was Jim Hickman, who divided his time between the bag and the outfield and put together a season that was completely out of character. The man who, in eight previous seasons, had never hit more than 21 homers in any single year nor driven in more than 57 runs nor batted over .257 suddenly erupted to produce 32 home runs, 115 RBIs, and a .315 batting average.

Johnny Callison was obtained from the Phillies to fill one of those aching outfield holes, but the veteran's best days were behind him. Having traded Selma for Callison, the Cubs once more found themselves short a

Ernie Banks: The trail was winding down.

starting pitcher, and in June they filled the vacancy by purchasing right-hander Milt Pappas from the Braves. (Milt is noted in baseball history as the only man to have 200 career wins but never a twenty-game season.)

Jim Hickman (1968–1973): 1970 was his dream year.

ments, and for Ernie Banks it was home-run number 500 on May 12. For Billy Williams, it was yearlong achievement. The Chicago left fielder extended his consecutive game streak to 1,117 before benching himself on September 3 (Williams's record was broken by Steve Garvey in 1983); Billy also turned in a prime year with 42 home runs (a Cub record by a left-handed batter), a league high of 205 hits, and a .322 batting average. Santo had 26 homers and 114 RBIs.

Jenkins made it four straight charmed seasons with a 22–16 ledger, setting still another club strikeout record with 274. Holtzman was 17–11, Hands 18–15, and Pappas 10–8.

What no doubt hurt the team more than anything else in 1970 was the loss of Randy Hundley to a knee injury for half the season.

The Cubs were at the top of the league for sixty-four consecutive days in 1970, from April 23 through June 24, but then began stubbing their toes and stumbling toward their eventual second-place finish. A twelve-game losing streak in late June, one short of the team record, sent them into their tailspin. As late as September 4, they were in a virtual first-place tie, but then they played 12–13 ball the rest of the way, while the Pirates were 17–9. For the second straight year, the Cubs had been torpedoed in September.

Veteran hitters generally go into the twilight on the wings of milestone achieve-

Milt Pappas (1970–1973), who won 209 games in his career but never more than 17 in a season.

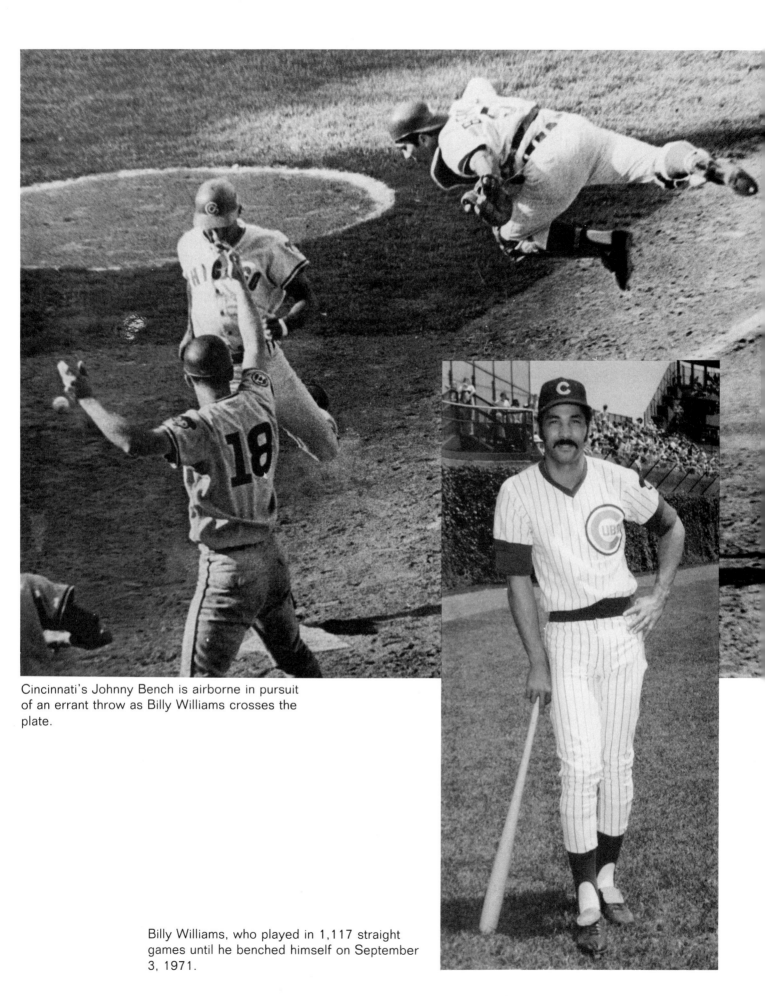

Cincinnati's Johnny Bench is airborne in pursuit of an errant throw as Billy Williams crosses the plate.

Billy Williams, who played in 1,117 straight games until he benched himself on September 3, 1971.

Ferguson Jenkins was a twenty-game winner for the Cubs six years in a row.

The 1971 campaign saw another repeat of the team's late-season hex. After a double-header sweep of Houston on August 20, the Cubs were 4½ games behind first-place Pittsburgh, were beginning a long home stand, and seemed primed to make their move. Instead, they lost 18 of their next 24 and ended the season tied for third place with the Mets, 14 games behind.

As always seemed to happen sooner or later on a Durocher-led team, the manager had his critics. After much sulking and grumbling, the turmoil reached the surface in late August, moving Phil Wrigley to address the dissenters in a full-page newspaper ad. The boss backed his skipper to the hilt, saying, among other things, that "the Dump Durocher Clique might as well give up."

Leo, who occasionally would offload blame,

had been making some unflattering public remarks about some of his players. The team, smarting under late-season disappointments, was not in a mood to hear the skipper going public with their faults.

At a team "clear the air" meeting on August 23, Durocher asked the players to speak their minds. Joe Pepitone, recently acquired from Houston, and Pappas told the skipper that his criticism of younger players created tension and were counterproductive. Holtzman also suggested that Leo's lack of tact was harmful (the pitcher, who had won just one game after June, had endured a skinful of Leo's barbs). When Durocher suggested that Santo was trying to glorify himself, the third baseman had to be restrained from restructuring Leo's profile. After the meeting, according to Ferguson Jenkins, "the unspoken agreement between Leo and the players was to talk to each other only if the situation demanded it."

The dissension hurt, but nothing hurt the 1971 Cubs more than the loss of Hundley, as the star catcher crumbled under further knee problems, entering just nine games. He was replaced by a committee of five different catchers, none of whom was his equal.

Outside of Jenkins (24–13) and Beckert (.342), no one had a standout year. Williams hit well—28 homers, 93 RBIs, .301 average—but this production was below his high marks of 1970. Hickman also dropped considerably from his onetime-only 1970 year, and even Santo began tailing off, his 21 homers and 88 RBIs being his lowest since 1962. Pepitone batted .307 and hit 16 homers, but Joe annoyed a number of teammates with his flamboyant ways. An arthritic knee helped put a wrap on Ernie Banks's Hall of Fame career, and the most popular Cub of all bowed out with 3 home runs and a .193 average in thirty-nine games.

Pappas turned in a solid 17–14 season, but Hands slipped to 12–18 and Holtzman to 9–15, though Ken brightened his summer with his second no-hitter, a 1–0 stifling of the Reds on June 3.

Ron Santo, poised to snatch the throw and lay
the tag on Montreal's sliding Rusty Staub.

Glenn Beckert batted .342 in 1971.

Jose Cardenal (1972–1977), who played for nine different teams in his seventeen-year big-league career.

Showing little faith in his bullpen, which was still headed by Phil Regan and which recorded just 13 saves, Leo drove his starters to 75 complete games, an inordinately high number for the times (no National League team has come close to it since). Jenkins hurled 30 complete games and worked 325 innings, going over 300 for the fourth year in a row. The big right-hander's sterling work was recognized after the season when he became the first Cub pitcher to win the Cy Young Award.

Intent on getting the outfielders the team needed so badly, Holland swung a couple of deals soon after the end of the season. He obtained the speedy Jose Cardenal from Milwaukee in exchange for three young players,

one of whom, right-hander Jim Colborn, soon became a twenty-game winner for the Brewers. He then sent Holtzman to Oakland for Rick Monday.

The team could part with a top starter because they had confidence in a pair of young right-handers who were about to break into the rotation, Burt Hooton and Rick Reuschel. Pitching, in fact, turned out to be the club's strong suit in 1972. Jenkins won 20 for the sixth straight time (20–12), and Pappas delivered another strong season with a 17–7 record. Hands was 11–8, Hooton 11–14, and Reuschel 10–8. Hooton, making his first start of the season on April 16, electrified the Wrigley crowd with a 4–0 no-hitter over the Phillies. On September 2 at Wrigley, Pappas

Outfielder Rick Monday (1972–1976), who was later traded to Los Angeles for Bill Buckner and Ivan DeJesus.

Burt Hooton (1971–1975). Tommy Lasorda nicknamed him "Happy" because he rarely smiled, but he couldn't resist on April 16, 1972, after pitching a no-hitter against the Phillies.

was even better. In throwing an 8–0 no-hitter against San Diego, the tall right-hander retired the first twenty-six men he faced, walked pinch-hitter Larry Stahl on a near-miss three-and-two pitch, and then retired the next batter. This gave Cubs' pitchers four no-hitters in three years.

Billy Williams, National League batting champion in 1972.

Jose Cardenal is making a valiant effort, but Montreal's
Gary Carter is tagging him out at home.

The estimable Billy Williams gave the team
its first batting champion since Phil Cavarretta in 1945, when he tagged league pitching
for a .333 mark, brightened with 37 homers
and 122 RBIs. Santo batted .302, but his
power decline continued with just 17 homers.
Cardenal batted .291, but Monday struggled
at .249. Hundley was back behind the plate,
though not the same player he had been, a
fact borne out by his .218 batting average.

On July 24, 1972, the six-and-a-half-year
reign of Leo Durocher, longest in consecutive
years of any Cub manager since Frank

Chance, came to a sudden end. The official
wording that accompanied the announce-
ment of Leo's departure was vague as to
whether he had been nudged or if the whole
thing was his own idea. Leo said he was not
being fired; the team said he was "stepping
aside." It sounded like a case of a man being
politely asked either to step away or be run
over by a truck.

Durocher's replacement was Carroll
("Whitey") Lockman, who had played first
base on Leo's 1951 "miracle" New York Giants, and who had lately been working for the

Cubs in various capacities, most recently as director of player development. The Cub players knew and liked him.

Under Durocher in 1972, the Cubs had been 46–44 (.511), while under Lockman they sailed to a 39–26 record (.600), a considerable improvement but not enough to land the club higher than second, 11 games behind the Pirates.

Over the past six years, the Cubs had finished third, third, second, second, third, and second. Coming after twenty straight years of second-division interment, this was almost like a golden age, or at least a gilded age. But too many soaring hopes had gone off into the blue and never been seen again, and now an air of frustration was setting in. There was a feeling that over the past six years a pennant should have been won, at least once. The team had put plenty of talent on the field; but talent was perishable, and now some of the best of it was fading for the Cubs. Banks had retired; Santo seemed burned out at thirty-two; Hundley and Beckert were slowed by injuries; Holtzman had been traded, and Hands shortly would be.

If this upbeat six years had not produced a pennant, it had at least thrown some refreshing rainbows across the Wrigley Field sky and revived winning baseball. Disappointed or not, Cub fans would soon be looking back at those teams and their stars with a certain wistfulness as another turnaround in club history began.

Skipper Whitey Lockman might be giving a sign, or he might be thinking of giving one.

Randy Hundley *(left)* and Burt Hooton.

In his one full season as manager in 1973, Lockman finished fifth with a 77–84 record but, because of the vagaries of divisional play, almost won a title. Going into the season's final week, five of the six Eastern Division clubs had a shot at the top, with the Mets finally winning despite an 82–79 record. Lockman's club, which had been in first place as late as the All-Star break, were 5 behind at the finish, thanks to a July-August blackout that saw them bumble to a 17–37 record.

Don Kessinger has just forced fellow shortstop Gene Alley of the Pirates at second base and is firing to first in hopes of completing a double play.

Bill Madlock (1974–1976). He had a pretty deadly aim with that thing.

The 1973 season had a last-hurrah quality to it, for after its completion many of the club's longtime stars departed. You could see the skid marks behind Santo's career now, the veteran third baseman dropping to 20 homers, 77 RBIs, and a .267 batting average. Williams and Beckert also fell off offensively. After six straight seasons of twenty or more wins, Jenkins dropped to 14–16, while Pappas slipped to 7–12.

Rick Monday led the team with 26 home runs, and Jose Cardenal topped the hitters at .303. Hooton (14–17) and Reuschel (14–15) matched Jenkins in victories, and Bob Locker, acquired from Oakland in exchange for out-

Left-handed reliever Darold Knowles (1975–1976).

fielder Billy North, was the most frequent visitor from the bullpen, appearing in 63 games and chalking up 18 wins.

It was clear after the 1973 season, in which the Cubs were tenth in batting and runs scored, that it was time for a new cast. It was a hard and unsentimental broom that swept through the Chicago clubhouse: Jenkins, Santo, Beckert, Hundley, Pappas, and Hickman were gone before the opening of the 1974 season, and Williams soon after its close. The only man remaining from the contenders of the late sixties and early seventies was Kessinger.

210

Bill Bonham (1971–1977).

The club's 1974 rotation featured Bill Bonham (11–22), Reuschel (13–12), and Hooton (7–11). Steve Stone, who had come from the White Sox with three other players for Santo (who played just one disappointing season on the other side of town and then retired), was the only starter with a winning record (8–6).

This first rebuilding attempt was a complete failure. The team finished last with a 66–96 record, were ninth in batting (.251), eleventh in pitching (4.28), and made by far the most errors (199), the most by a Cub team since 1950.

After ninety-three games, Lockman relinquished the managerial post and returned to his job as director of player development. Whitey was replaced by his third-base coach, Jim Marshall.

The forty-two-year-old Marshall had had a modest five-year playing career, during which

Cub fans were puzzled by the Jenkins swap, which sent the great pitcher to the Texas Rangers for two little-known players, infielder-outfielder Vic Harris and third baseman Bill Madlock.

"That trade was no accident," Cub coach Pete Reiser said later. "We wanted Madlock. We knew just how good he was."

Madlock was, in fact, the brightest light on the 1974 Cubs, leading the team with a .313 batting average, compiled primarily with singles and doubles (he hit 9 homers). Monday (.294) and Cardenal (.293) also had good years, while the thirty-six-year-old Billy Williams ended his sixteen-year Cub career with a .280 season. In October the longtime favorite was traded to Oakland for second baseman Manny Trillo and pitchers Darold Knowles and Bob Locker (who had been traded back to Oakland after the 1973 season).

Catcher George Mitterwald (1974–1977).

The star of Chicago was Madlock, who banged away steadily all year and won the batting title with a .354 average, best for a Cub since Cavarretta's .355 crown in 1945. Cardenal generated the best of his eighteen big-league seasons (spent with nine different clubs) with a .317 average. Outfielder Jerry Morales led with 91 RBIs. First baseman Andre Thornton, soon to be traded to Montreal, batted .293 and hit 18 homers.

The team was fifth in batting in 1975 (.259) and third in runs (712), a decided improvement, but the pitching was woeful, the staff's 4.57 ERA by far the league's worst. Despite being hit hard, right-hander Ray Burris managed a 15–10 year, but Reuschel dropped to 11–17 (he was the ninth Cub pitcher since 1946 to lead the league in losses), and Bonham was 13–15. Stone again posted a winning mark at 12–8.

Jim Marshall, who played for the Cubs from 1958 to 1959 and later managed the team from 1974 to 1976.

he had put in some time at first base for the Cubs in 1958 and 1959. Later he had played in Japan for several years, then had come back and taken on a string of minor-league managerial jobs for the Cubs, graduating to coach and now skipper of the big team. Following Chance, Grimm, and Cavarretta, he was the fourth ex-Cub first baseman to manage the team in the twentieth century (after first baseman Anson had run the team for nineteen years at the end of the nineteenth century).

Marshall edged the club up a notch in 1975, earning a fifth-place tie with Montreal. The team's best work was done early in the year; they were in first place into early June, then took a plunge and spent the rest of the summer trying to keep the water under their chins.

A proud Bill Madlock is holding the John A. "Bud" Hillerich Memorial Award presented to him for winning the 1975 National League batting title.

Jerry Morales (1974–1977, 1981–1983), who hit steadily for the Cubs.

The club made an unfortunate trade of pitchers early in the season, sending Hooton to the Dodgers for right-hander Eddie Solomon and lefty Geoff Zahn. Neither man contributed much to the Cubs (Zahn, a junkballer, later became a steady winner in the American League with the Twins and Angels), while Hooton went on to become a bulwark on three Dodger pennant winners.

It would have been nice if the Cubs had been able to mark the hundredth anniversary of their entry into the National League with a winning season, but unfortunately the centennial year came during another downswing for the club. Marshall brought home a squad that played to the same 75–87 record as in 1975, this time finishing fourth. Outside of Bill Madlock, this was not a distinguished Cub team. Madlock not only won his second

consecutive batting crown with a .339 average but did it with flair and drama, going 4 for 4 on the last day of the season to wrest the title from Cincinnati's Ken Griffey. Griffey had chosen to sit down on that final day and freeze what he assumed would be his league-leading average, but when word of Madlock's relentless hitting reached Cincinnati, Griffey was forced into the lineup. Madlock kept tagging the ball; Griffey did not. When the day was over, Madlock was the title holder by three points.

Aside from this bit of theater, which Cub fans had to wait all season to enjoy, there was not much to cheer about at Wrigley in the centennial summer. Cardenal finished up at .299, and Monday hit 32 homers. Reuschel was 14–12; Burris, 15–13.

Andre Thornton (1973–1976), who later went on to have some solid seasons with the Cleveland Indians.

Ray Burris (1973–1979), twice a 15-game winner for the Cubs.

Kessinger had been traded to the Cardinals, replaced by a tandem of Mick Kelleher and Dave Rosello, neither of whom was good enough to claim the shortstop job on a regular basis. The most significant addition to the team in 1976 was a twenty-three-year-old right-handed relief specialist named Bruce Sutter. Featuring a variation on the forkball that was dubbed a "split-fingered fastball," a pitch that dropped abruptly as it approached the plate—as much as a foot, according to

some people—the rookie appeared in 52 games, had a 6–3 record, 10 saves, and a 2.71 ERA. In 83 innings he gave up just 63 hits, fanning 73 and walking 26.

The Cubs installed a new manager in 1977, Herman Franks. As manager of the San Francisco Giants, Franks had finished in second place four years in a row (1965–68); the ex-catcher had served briefly as a coach under Durocher during Leo's reign as Cub skipper.

After winning two batting titles, Madlock

Rick Monday became a national hero when he prevented two protesters from burning an American flag on the outfield grass at Dodger Stadium. The incident occurred during a game on April 25, 1976.

A familiar sight: Bruce Sutter warming up in the Wrigley bullpen. The super reliever pitched for Chicago from 1976 to 1980.

Cubs manager Herman Franks *(right)* doing the managers' war dance after being booted out of a game. Umpire Doug Harvey is unmoved by the ritual.

asked for a contract that the Cubs considered exorbitant, reportedly $1 million over five years (a few years later, that money would seem quaint). The team rejected his demands and dispatched Bill to the Giants for outfielder Bobby Murcer and third baseman Steve Ontiveros. Another transaction sent Rick Monday to the Dodgers for first baseman Bill Buckner and shortstop Ivan DeJesus. Three of the four infielders had now been replaced, with only second baseman Manny Trillo remaining.

Ontiveros led the 1977 regulars with a .299 average, though part-time outfielder Gregg Gross was the overall leader at .322. The

Ivan DeJesus (1977–1981), for five years Chicago's regular shortstop.

work from lefty Willie Hernandez, who seven years later would win both MVP and Cy Young honors for helping the Detroit Tigers to the pennant.

Thanks largely to Sutter, the Cubs got off to a strong start in 1977, leading the league for sixty-nine days, until August 4 (the day Sutter went on the twenty-one day disabled list). A gradual decline set in, and when the last shot had been fired, the team was 81–81, nestled in fourth place.

Earlier in 1977, on April 12, an era in Chicago baseball came to an end with the death of Philip K. Wrigley at the age of eighty-two. The man who had owned the team for forty-two years was genuinely mourned. Wrigley was a name synonymous with baseball own-

team's average of .266 was its highest since 1945, but averages were generally up around the league. Murcer delivered the long ball, as he had throughout his career, hitting a team-high 27 home runs.

With a 20–12 ledger, Reuschel was the club's first 20-game winner since Jenkins in 1972. Meanwhile, Sutter blazed to high-profile stardom in 1977; some people referred to the Cubs as virtually "a one-man team." Despite losing some time to shoulder problems, the ace reliever won 7 games and saved 31 others, firing his almost unhittable gravity pitch so effectively that in 107 innings he gave up just 69 hits, striking out 129 and walking 23, recording a flinty 1.35 ERA. The team also received some splendid bullpen

Manny Trillo (1975–1978), who gave the Cubs some excellent work at second base.

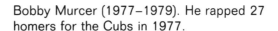

Bobby Murcer (1977–1979). He rapped 27 homers for the Cubs in 1977.

ership, the way Mack was in Philadelphia; Comiskey, with the Chicago White Sox; Yawkey, in Boston; Griffith, in Washington and Minnesota; and Stoneham, in New York and San Francisco. Each in his own way had personalized his stewardship and observed his own singular sentimentality.

Phil Wrigley had generally been popular with his players; his approaches to improving his team had not always been the correct ones, but they had always been genuine and generous. Because he wanted to retain the aesthetics of Wrigley Field and had been concerned with the nocturnal tranquillity of the

Rick Reuschel (1972–1981, 1983–1984). He was a twenty-game winner in 1977.

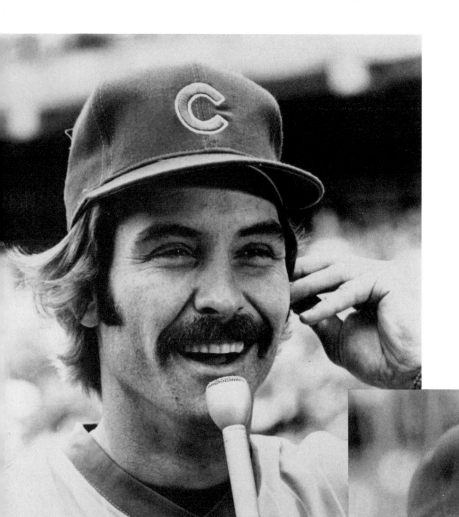

surrounding neighborhood, he was the last holdout against night ball in his park. Not everyone agreed, but Wrigley's reasons were understood and respected.

When he died the game's economic structure was beginning to change. Player salaries were about to soar so high that contracts came down with icicles on them. It was a change Wrigley disapproved of; indeed, he had disposed of star players Madlock and Monday because he felt their salary demands were excessive and unrealistic. In his opinion, "No ballplayer is worth more than $100,000 a year, and I'm not sure they're worth that much."

Dave Kingman (1978–1980). He was not always this cordial with the media.

Bill Buckner (1977–1984). In 1980 he became the Cubs' fourth batting champion in nine years.

An aerial view of Wrigley Field.

That was the conservative Wrigley, a reflection of his own formative years in the game, when player salaries averaged around $5,000 a year. But there had also been an innovative side to Phil Wrigley. The idea of rotating coaches to manage his team had been a mistake, but the concept had been radical. Wrigley had also been a pioneer in insisting that the broadcast of Cub games be made available to as wide an audience as possible. He did this not necessarily for profit but because he believed baseball belonged to its fans, particularly those who were unable to get to the ballpark. (Accounts of Cub games were broadcast over radio as early as 1925.)

Ownership of the Cubs passed to P. K.'s son William, who faced a burden of heavy inheritance taxes. The younger Wrigley's first response to those who advised that he sell the club was negative; however, the twilight of Wrigley ownership of the Chicago Cubs had begun to fall.

In the sometimes surrealistic world of divisional play, Herman Franks's club won fewer games in 1978 (79) than in 1977 but still managed to finish a rung higher, in third place. They did this with the slugging help of their first reentry free agent signee, Dave Kingman, who was the only Cub to homer in double figures. The team hit just 72 home runs, fewest for a Wrigley Field unit since 1947, and of these Kingman launched 28.

The Cubs led the league with a .264 batting average (the first Cub team to lead since 1945), sparked by Bill Buckner's .323. DeJesus stole 41 bases, most by a Cub player since Kiki Cuyler's 43 in 1929.

The club's chances in 1978 were sabotaged by poor pitching, with Reuschel (14–15) the only man on the staff to win in double figures, though Mike Krukow was 9–3. Not quite as scintillating as the year before, Sutter still managed to save 27 games, posting an 8–10 record.

Despite their spotty pitching, the Cubs were in first place for a month, starting on May 24. Their inability to handle the eventual division winners, the Phillies, cost them dearly in 1978. Between June 23 and July 2, they lost 8 of 9 to the Phillies, tumbled to second place, and never rebounded.

The adage that all statistics are relative was reinforced in 1979. The Cubs won more games than in 1978 (80), hit more home runs (135), scored more runs (706), batted higher (.269), and had a lower ERA (3.88)—and finished down two spots, in fifth place.

Dave Kingman gave the team an explosive year, hitting 48 home runs to become the first Cub since Banks in 1960 to lead the league. The big man also drove in 115 runs (the team's first 100-RBI man since Billy Williams in 1972), as well as putting his big swing on display with 131 strikeouts, most in the league. Kingman batted a career-best .288, making him one of five .280 hitters in the regular lineup, including Buckner, DeJesus, Ontiveros, and rookie outfielder Scot Thompson (in his only productive year).

Reuschel topped the staff with a big 18–12 season, veteran Lynn McGlothen (acquired from the Giants the year before) was 13–14, and Dennis Lamp, 11–10. Sutter saved 37 games (tops in the league) and was paced in the pen by right-hander Dick Tidrow, who was 11–5.

Chicago's contest of the year in 1979 came on May 17, when the Cubs and Phillies played a game reminiscent of the 26–23 slugfest put on by their professional ancestors in 1922. This time it was a 23–22 barrel of fun, in which the Cubs came back from a 17–6 deficit only to lose on a ten-inning home run by Mike Schmidt (who had popped 4 homers in another ten-inning Wrigley game in 1976). Eleven home runs were hit by both sides, tying a major-league record for two clubs in an extra-inning game. Kingman swatted 3 of them while driving in 6 runs, and Buckner drove in 7 runs, all in a losing cause. As far as the record book was concerned, for the Cubs it was just another tough one-run loss.

Going into September, the Cubs had a fair shot at the division title, trailing by 5½ games, but then a major capsize occurred: 14 losses in 17 games and a rapid descent to the lower depths. With a week to go in the season, Herman Franks resigned, and coach Joey Amalfitano finished up.

The decade that had begun with such high hopes ended with a thud. There was, however, a note of postseason glory: Bruce Sutter's superb season earned him the Cy Young Award.

E·L·E·V·E·N

BETTER DAYS

AS the page turned on a new decade, Cub fans felt left out and frustrated. Their team had not had a winner of any kind since 1945, not even a division winner. They were still coming out to Wrigley, more than a million strong every summer, but now it seemed more because of fidelity than hope.

The 1980 club was at least merciful; after winning a few games in the early going, it quickly sank to its level of futility, by midseason dropping to last place and maintaining stubborn and permanent possession of the cellar for the rest of the year.

The new manager was Preston Gomez, who had mastered the art of finishing last while managing at San Diego and Houston. (In seven seasons managing the Padres, Astros, and Cubs, Gomez led only one team that did not finish in last place.) When he became skipper of the Cubs, it was as though some sort of mission had been accomplished, and he was duly fired, on July 25. His replacement was Amalfitano, who steered the leaky boat to port with a final 64–98 record, one of the worst in the team's history.

Injuries had cut Kingman's playing time in half, leaving Dave with just 18 home runs; the big man's often boorish personality had just about worn out his welcome, and he was traded to the Mets the following winter. Outfielder Jerry Martin led the team with 23 homers and 73 RBIs but batted just .227; he was traded also, to the Giants.

The one man in the lineup to have an outstanding season was Bill Buckner, who that

year split his time between first base and the outfield. Bill's .324 batting average was good enough to lead the league in 1980, giving the team its sixth batting champion since 1901.

One of the interesting things about the 1980 Cubs was the makeup of their bullpen. In addition to Sutter, who led the league with

Joey Amalfitano, Cub manager in 1980 and 1981.

Outfielder/first baseman Larry Biittner (1976–1980).

28 saves, the Cubs had: Dick Tidrow, who had a fine year as he tied Abernathy's team record with 84 appearances; hard-throwing right-hander Bill Caudill, who was to become a star reliever in the American League for Seattle; Willie Hernandez, who had a wretched year for the Cubs in 1980 but would become a star with the Tigers; and the man who was about to replace Sutter and hoist his own star, the big, hard-throwing right-hander, Lee Smith.

Smith and the others were about to get their chance, for on December 9, 1980, the Cubs stunned their fans by trading Sutter to the Cardinals for third baseman Ken Reitz, utility man Ty Waller, and outfielder Leon Durham. Of the three only Durham would contribute much to the Chicago cause.

The reason behind the trade was money—

that is, Sutter had demanded too much of it. The ace reliever had taken a salary dispute to arbitration and been awarded $700,000, which the club thought excessive. The idea of dealing a star player because his salary seemed too high was now like a ghostly wind out of the past. And one of the last names associated with that past was about to depart from the game.

Unwilling to cope with the financial structure of baseball's new age and still struggling with inheritance taxes, William Wrigley ended his family's sixty-five-year, three-generation association with the Chicago Cubs. On June 16, 1981, the sale of the team to the *Chicago Tribune* Company for an estimated $20.5 million was announced.

Ironically, the passing from the game of one of its most familiar names followed by a few days more evidence of baseball's new age—the player strike. What two world wars and an economic depression had been unable to do, baseball did to itself. On June 12, the players walked off the job and began a fifty-day strike. With the average major-league salary just under $200,000 (it would more than double in a few years), the point of the strike was lost on most fans, who waited impatiently for the return of their favorite summertime diversion. Agreement was finally reached on July 31 and play resumed on August 10.

With their season in a shambles, the baseball establishment decided to try to pique interest by creating a split season, declaring all first-place teams as of June 12 winners of the first half; these would play the winners of the second half in divisional playoffs that would precede the regular pennant playoffs.

This was as crack-brained a scheme as could have been devised, but it did not affect the Cubs one way or the other. Amalfitano's men finished last in the first half and fifth in the second.

Through all the distractions, Bill Buckner batted .311, outfielder Steve Henderson (who had come from the Mets in exchange for Kingman) was a .293 hitter, Leon Durham hit .293, and Jerry Morales, .286. Despite these highly presentable marks, the team batting average of .236 was the league's lowest. Mike Krukow, 9–9, was the team's top pitcher in the fractured season

The man selected by the *Tribune* Company to run their new investment was Dallas Green, who took over at the end of the 1981 season. Green had had a nondescript playing career, pitching for three teams (primarily the

Backup catcher Tim Blackwell, who was with the Cubs from 1978 to 1981.

Bill Buckner on the move.

Phillies) from 1960–67, leaving with a 20–22 record. But at six feet five inches, he was never overlooked. Tall, handsome, and bright, with leadership qualities that were appreciated by the Phillies, he was given jobs in the Philadelphia farm system and front office and in 1979 took over as manager. In 1980 he drove his team to the world championship. In 1981 his club had won the first half of the splintered season, then been eliminated in the divisional playoffs. Now he had been hired to run the Cubs.

This was no mere new broom in the front office but, rather, a bulldozer. Green announced that he was not there to make friends but to win ball games. This was a sound policy, for if he won ball games, he would not lack for friends; if he did not win ball games, it would not matter if he had the sweetest of dispositions.

Mike Krukow (1976–1981).

8, 1981, Green finessed the versatile Keith Moreland away from Philadelphia for Mike Krukow. Then, on January 27, 1982, he traded Ivan DeJesus to the Phillies for short-stop Larry Bowa, a record-setting defensive shortstop. There was also a "throw-in" on the part of the Phillies, twenty-two-year-old in-fielder Ryne Sandberg.

The 1982 Cubs began poorly, suffering a thirteen-game losing streak that began at the end of May, but played well in August and September. Despite a fifth-place finish, the signs were positive.

Recovering from a 1-for-31 beginning, Sandberg batted .271. The youngster played most of the year at third base, then in September took over second base, where he would remain, soon to rival Johnny Evers and Billy Herman in the history of Chicago Cubs

Green began by agitating for the installa-tion of lights at Wrigley Field. He would not succeed, but the forces he helped set in mo-tion would finally result in illuminating the old ballpark in 1988.

What Green did, and most effectively, was begin to make the Cubs resemble an exten-sion of the Phillies. He installed as manager former Phillies coach Lee Elia. Elia's brief big-league playing career had consisted of eighty games with the White Sox in 1966 and fif-teen with the Cubs in 1968. Lee was the fif-teenth active or former Cub player to manage the team, going back to Frank Chance.

Green knew the Phillie personnel as well as anyone, and when he began dealing with his former employers he raided their roster with almost surgical precision. On December

Dallas Green, when he was a pitcher with the Phillies in the early 1960s.

(TOP LEFT) Green's first choice for Cubs manager, Lee Elia, who ran the team in 1982 and 1983. He played in a handful of games with the Cubs as an infielder in 1968.

(TOP RIGHT) Keith Moreland (1982–1987).

(BOTTOM) Larry Bowa (1982–1985), one of the many Philadelphia players Green finessed away from his former employers.

Ryne Sandberg, the Cubs' greatest second baseman since Billy Herman.

brought home to Chicago, after eight years in the American League. Now thirty-eight years old, Jenkins, as ever, took his regular turn and gave the Cubs a 14–15 year. No other pitcher on the staff won as many.

Except for a mound corps that would be almost entirely rebuilt, the team that would win the division title in 1984 was almost fully in place in 1983. Outside of a rather ragged pitching staff, it was a very strong Cub team that finished fifth in 1983, outscoring every

second basemen. Buckner had another strong year, rapping out 201 hits, driving in 105 runs, and batting .306. Durham contributed 22 homers (most on the team) and batted .312. Moreland and catcher Jody Davis were .261 hitters.

Reuschel had been dealt to the Yankees the year before, and the staff had a new leader. His was a familiar face: Ferguson Jenkins had opted for free agency and been

Jody Davis (1981–1988).

team in the league but one, placing second in home runs (140), first in slugging (.401), and first in fielding (.982), thanks to a team-record low of 115 errors.

Sandberg and Bowa, each leading in fielding, were dazzling at second and short, and Ron Cey, acquired from the Dodgers for a pair of minor leaguers, provided power at third base (24 homers, 90 RBIs). Rookie Mel Hall was in center, Keith Moreland was in right, and Leon Durham in left, giving the outfield three solid bats. Jody Davis caught 150 games and batted .271 with 24 homers and 84 RBIs.

The team was 38–41 at the All-Star break, but with the caprices of divisional play, that nondescript record had them only 4 games out of first place. The second half, however, saw them play with consistent mediocrity: 12–17 in July, 12–17 in August, and 12–18 in October.

The problem lay with the pitching. Right-hander Chuck Rainey, picked up from the Red Sox, won the most (14–13) but had a 4.48 ERA (the team ERA of 4.07 was the league's worst in 1983). Left-hander Steve Trout, who came to the Cubs in a crosstown swap with the White Sox, was 10–14, and right-hander Dick Ruthven, whom Green had lassoed from the Phillies for Willie Hernandez, was 12–9. In his final big-league season, Jenkins went 6–9 and retired with a career 284 victories. Rick Reuschel was back, having been dropped by the Yankees, but contributed little. (The Cubs would let him get away again the next year, and after overcoming some physical problems, the bulky right-hander would resurface as an ace pitcher with the Pirates and then the Giants.)

Despite a 4–10 won–lost record, Lee Smith had 29 saves and a 1.65 ERA. The most frequent arrivee from the pen was the veteran Bill Campbell, who pitched in 82 games, two short of the club record. Smith, Campbell, Warren Brusstar, Craig Lefferts, and Mike Proly each appeared in fifty or more games, thanks to the starters' league-low 9 complete games.

A frustrated Lee Elia popped off in the

Ron Cey (1983–1986). The former Dodger third baseman did some solid hitting for the Cubs.

clubhouse after an April game, his target not his players but the Cub fans. Elia's tirade, which was taped by a reporter, became a classic. The most memorable quote was "Eighty-five percent of the people in this country work. The other 15 percent come out here"—he meant Wrigley Field—"and boo my players." After that, the clock began ticking for Lee Elia, and on August 22 he joined that 15 percent. He was replaced by front-office executive Charlie Fox on an interim basis.

For the team's new manager, Green chose Jim Frey, a man of considerable experience. A career minor-league outfielder who had

Middle-inning reliever Warren Brusstar, who gave the Cubs some good work from 1983 to 1985.

Dick Ruthven (1983–1986), another man Green plucked from the Philadelphia roster.

never made it to the majors, Frey had managed in the minors, coached for a decade under Earl Weaver at Baltimore, then taken over the Kansas City Royals and won a pennant in 1980, only to be defeated in the World Series by Green's Phillies. Canned in KC in 1981, he signed on as batting coach for the Mets and from there was hired to manage the Cubs.

Confident that with some judicious additions his fifth-place club could make it to the top in 1984, Green went to work. With one stroke he was able to improve his outfield by bamboozling the Phillies out of Gary Matthews and Bob Dernier, sending his favorite trading partners catcher Mike Diaz (who never played for the Phillies) and a worn-out Bill Campbell.

Then, turning to his club's weak link, its pitching, on May 25, 1984, Green sent first baseman Bill Buckner to the Red Sox in exchange for right-hander Dennis Eckersley. On June 14 Green applied the finishing touch. To Cleveland went outfielders Mel Hall and Joe Carter and pitchers Don Schulze and Darryl Banks, in return for pitchers Rick Sutcliffe and George Frazier and catcher Ron Hassey.

The big man in the deal, as far as the Cubs were concerned, was Sutcliffe. The tall right-hander had been Rookie of the Year with the Dodgers in 1979, then fallen from grace in Los Angeles and gone on to Cleveland, where

Bob Dernier (1984–1987), who stole 45 bases for the Cubs in 1984.

Jim Frey.

he won 17 games in 1983. Sporting a 4–5 record at the time of the trade, he became almost unbeatable with the Cubs for the rest of the year, chalking up a 16–1 record (at one point reeling off 14 straight wins) and winning the Cy Young Award. He was only the fourth pitcher ever to win 20 games in one season while pitching in both leagues. Fittingly, the last to do it was another man who helped the Cubs to a first-place finish, Hank Borowy in 1945.

The deal was not the swindle it first appeared to be, as Hall developed into a decent hitter in the American League and Carter soon became a premier hitter with the Indi-

Gary ("Sarge") Matthews (1984–1987).

Dennis Eckersley (1984–1986), a starter for the Cubs, later became a sterling reliever for the Oakland Athletics.

With Sutcliffe, Trout, Eckersley, Dick Ruthven, and Scott Sanderson doing most of the starting, and Lee Smith blazing out of the bullpen, Frey led his troops into battle.

The Cubs' most stubborn opponents for the top of the division were the New York Mets, who were flying on the wings of Dwight Gooden's 17–9 rookie season.

The Cubs were 12–8 in April and at the end of the month found themselves in a tie for first place with the Mets. The two teams then began kicking the top spot back and forth, neither able to shake off the other. At the end of June, the Cubs were 42–34, the Mets 38–33, a 1½-game lead for the Cubs.

The National League's 1984 Cy Young Award winner, Rick Sutcliffe, who was almost perfect at 16–1.

First baseman Leon Durham (1981–1988).

ans. Nevertheless, it was a swap no Cub fan would ever take back.

Frey moved Durham to first base and went with an outfield of Matthews, Moreland, and Dernier. The rest of the infield consisted of Sandberg, Bowa, and Cey, with Davis behind the plate. These regulars went through the season virtually free of serious injuries, Bowa's 133 games being the fewest any of them played.

232

Scott Sanderson (1984–1989).

16–11 in September, winning the division by 6½ games over the Mets. They ended with a 96–65 record, best for a Cub team since 1945. The successful season attracted 2,104,219 fans, a new club record.

In what was probably the team's most memorable game of the 1984 season, Ryne Sandberg burst into the headlines and remained there for the rest of the year (and for years to come). The game was played at Wrigley Field on June 23. With his team losing to the Cardinals 9–8 in the bottom of the ninth, Sandberg hit a two-out home run to tie the score. In the top of the tenth, the Cardinals scored twice, only to have Sandberg again tie

The Mets tore into the month of July, winning 12 of their first 13, a pace that enabled them to take over first place. On July 27 the two contenders met to begin the first of two four-game sets that would be played over thirteen days.

As the first series opened, at Shea Stadium, the Mets led by 3½ games. After losing the first game to Gooden, the Cubs then took the next three, sending the Mets into a seven-game tailspin. On August 1 a Cub win over the Phillies put Frey's team in first place, where they would remain for the rest of the season. The Cubs seriously battered the Mets at Wrigley beginning on August 6, sweeping four straight from the New Yorkers. Historically a month laden with minefields for them, the Cubs were 20–10 in August and a strong

Steve Trout (1983–1987).

The Cubs' big righty in the pen, Lee Smith (1980–1987).

the game, this time with a 2-run homer. Both of these storybook home runs gained added cachet by being struck against Bruce Sutter. With Sandberg knocking in 7 runs overall, the Cubs won in eleven innings, 12–11.

More than any other player, Sandberg was the driving force behind the Cubs' division title in 1984. The handsome youngster who had been purloined from the Phillies batted .314; had 200 hits which included 36 doubles, 19 triples (best in the league), and 19 home runs; scored a league-high 114 runs; drove in 84; stole 32 bases; and was equally outstanding in the field, leading National League second basemen in assists (550) and fielding (.993), making only 6 errors (one over the record for fewest)—at one point he had 62 straight errorless games. He was a landslide winner of the MVP Award.

No other Cub batted over .300 (Matthews's .291 was next highest), but the squad

hit with consistency and timeliness, their 762 runs easily the most in the league. Six men in the lineup—Durham, Sandberg, Cey, Moreland, Matthews, and Davis—had 80 or more RBIs, with Cey's 97 tops; the stocky ex-Dodger also hit the most home runs, 25.

Outside of Sutcliffe, the pitching was less than brilliant but more than adequate; the staff ERA of 3.75 was bettered by nine other teams. Trout was 13–7, and Eckersley, 10–8. Sanderson (8–5) and Ruthven (6–10) each put in time on the disabled list. With Smith sealing Chicago victories with fire (9 wins, 33 saves), backed up by right-hander Tim Stoddard (10–6, 7 saves), the bullpen more than pulled their weight (no pun intended, but these two stalwarts weighed around four hundred fifty pounds between them).

For their first playoff series, the Cubs encountered the San Diego Padres, who were making their maiden voyage into postseason

Ryne Sandberg, the National League's MVP in 1984.

play. The series, then a best-of-five affair, opened at Wrigley with a thunderous 13–0 Cub victory, behind Sutcliffe. The tall right-hander was supported by 5 home runs, struck by Dernier, Matthews (2), Cey, and Sutcliffe himself. This battering was followed the next day by a 4–2 victory by Trout, with help from Smith in the ninth. The Cubs were now but one victory away from their first pennant in thirty-nine years.

In San Diego the Padres kept the under-taker at bay with a 7–1 victory, beating Eck-ersley with 3 runs in the fifth and 4 in the sixth. Game 4 was a Steve Garvey showcase. The Padre first baseman was 4 for 5, with 5 RBIs in an exciting game that went into the bottom of the ninth tied at 5–5. Sanderson had started for the Cubs, who had been bol-stered by home runs from Davis and Durham. With Smith on the mound, Padre Tony Gwynn singled with one out in the last of the ninth, and then Garvey capped his great game with a screaming home run into the bleachers in right-center, tying the series.

The Padres were now threatening to be-come the first National League team to re-cover from an 0–2 deficit and win a playoff series. The Cubs, however, were confident, and justly so, for they were sending to the mound their nearly unbeatable red-bearded giant, Sutcliffe.

Thanks to home runs by Durham and Da-vis, the Cubs jumped off to a 3–0 lead after two innings. San Diego relievers then stifled the Chicago bats, but it didn't seem to mat-ter, for Sutcliffe allowed just 2 infield singles through the first five innings.

The Padres broke through on Sutcliffe in the bottom of the sixth for 2 runs, narrowing the Chicago margin to 3–2. Then came the heartbreaking last of the seventh. A walk and a sacrifice put the tying run on second with one out. Pinch-hitter Tim Flannery then hit a grounder that went through Durham's legs, allowing the tying run to score. The Chicago nightmare had begun. The next batter, Alan Wiggins, punched a check-swing single into short left. Gwynn followed with more San Di-ego magic when his hard grounder took an erratic hop over Sandberg's shoulder and skipped into right-center for a 2-run double, giving the Padres a 5–3 lead. Garvey's single made it 6–3, which was the final score. An error, a check-swing hit, a bad hop, and the Cubs' fine season was soured at the finish line.

"We had them by the throat," a dejected Dallas Green said, "and let them get away."

With virtually the same team that had come so close in 1984, the Cubs went into the 1985 season with wounded pride and a determination to scale the mountain to the peak this time. But, sadly, they were un-done by an incredible epidemic of injuries that left their starting pitching in a shambles. On May 19 Sutcliffe tore a hamstring running out a grounder and was placed on the disabled

Thad Bosely (1983–1986), who led the league
with 20 pinch hits in 1985.

Shawon Dunston, who was groomed as Chicago's shortstop of the future.

Davey Lopes (1984–1986).

list. He soon had a lot of company: Trout (elbow), Eckersley (shoulder), Sanderson (knee), and Ruthven (broken toe) eventually joined him, effectively destroying the team's pitching. When he tried to return to action too soon, Sutcliffe hurt his arm and was lost for much of the rest of the season.

When the injuries began to strike, the team was just 2½ games out of first place. But then a thirteen-game losing streak (tying a club record) in June took them out of the race, and they ultimately lodged in fourth place.

The 1985 team hit 150 home runs to lead the league, with Sandberg (26), Cey (22), and Durham (21) heading the list. Sandberg was again superb, following his MVP season with a .305 batting average and 54 stolen bases, most by a Cub since Frank Chance's 57 in 1905. Moreland was the club's leading hitter with a .307 mark and also led the squad with 106 RBIs. The team also introduced Wrigley Field fans to its shortstop of the future, Shawon Dunston. After a shaky start, the youngster with the rocketlike throwing arm composed himself in the field and batted .260.

With Matthews and Dernier also missing

Rick Sutcliffe.

time because of injuries, the Cubs employed thirty-nine-year-old Davey Lopes in the outfield, and the veteran ex-Dodger put in a remarkable effort: in ninety-nine games he batted .284 and stole 47 bases.

Reflecting their many ailments, none of the starting pitchers achieved much glory in 1985, with Eckersley making the best showing at 11–7. For Sutcliffe, it was a post–Cy Young season of 8–8. What little there was to save was turned over to Smith, and once more the big bullet-throwing reliever did the job, winning 7 and saving 33.

Despite the team's struggling, the afterglow of 1984's great season was strong enough to attract a new club-record attendance of 2,161,534 to baseball's only all-sunshine park.

The Cubs hoped that the pitching that had fallen apart in 1985 would mesh in 1986 and unite with the team's good hitting to produce a happier season. Instead of improving, however, the rotation continued to deteriorate, logging the league's worst ERA (4.49). Suffering with an ailing shoulder, Sutcliffe dropped to 5–14, Eckersley was 6–11, and Trout became totally ineffective and had to be re-

Lee Smith.

became a manager without a job. Frey's replacement was former two-time New York Yankee skipper Gene Michael, who carried on to a quiet fifth-place finish.

After their championship season of 1984, the Cubs seemed to have become caught by a perverse and inexorable gravitational pull: from first place they went to fourth, fifth, and then in 1987 sixth. This was despite a league-high (and club-record) 209 home runs, most in the league since the Reds hit 221 in 1956. It was a robust home-run-hitting season throughout the major leagues, with baseballs flying out of parks in unprecedented numbers (3,813 in 1986 to 4,458 in 1987).

Although their team finished last, Cub fans in 1987 were lavishly entertained by the explosive hitting of Andre Dawson, who was,

Andre ("The Hawk") Dawson, who made a gift of himself to the Cubs in 1987, a year in which he hit 49 home runs and was voted the league's Most Valuable Player.

moved from the rotation. Among the starters only Sanderson won as many as 9 games (9–11), as the team failed for the first time to have a pitcher with at least ten victories (excluding the 1981 strike year). Smith remained unaffected by the busted wings around him, winning 9 and saving 31.

The team's 155 home runs led the league for the second straight year, with Matthews, Davis, and Durham hitting 20 or better. Sandberg continued to write the book at second base, winning a fourth straight Gold Glove as he tied a major-league record for fewest errors at his position (5) and set a National League fielding standard (.993).

In 1984 Jim Frey had been National League Manager of the Year; on June 12, 1986, he

quite literally, a gift to them from the rest of major-league baseball. Wanting to escape Montreal, where he had starred for ten years, and to play on natural grass to favor his aching knees, Dawson and other free agents found themselves victims of what an arbiter would later rule as collusion on the part of the big-league owners. The free agents received either no offers or offers not commensurate with their established market value. The frustrated Dawson then took a novel approach: his agent notified the Cubs that the outfielder wished to play for them and would sign a blank contract, with Dallas Green filling in the salary. Finding this proposition irresistible, and probably delighted by the windfall, Green filled in a salary of $500,000 (less than a third of what Dawson would have commanded in an open market), plus another few hundred thousand in incentives.

The Dawson transaction turned out to be a huge bargain for Chicago as Andre went on to lead the league with 49 home runs (hitting 15 of them in August, a Cub record for a single month) and 137 runs batted in. He became the first player from a last-place team to win a Most Valuable Player Award, the seventh time a Cub had been so honored.

Dawson's long-balling was abetted by Durham and Moreland, each with 27 homers. Veteran outfielder Jerry Mumphrey led the team with a .333 average, compiled in 309 at-bats. The club was hurt when Dunston went on the disabled list for two months in the heart of the season and was not adequately replaced.

The team enjoyed a resurgence by Sutcliffe, who rang up an 18–10 record (most wins in the league), despite going winless from July 29 to September 12, a dry spell that cost him a second Cy Young Award —he lost to Philadelphia's Steve Bedrosian by two points. Southpaw Jamie Moyer was the only other staff member to win in double figures, going 12–15 (with an inflated 5.10 ERA). Smith had some bumpy times coming out of the bullpen, as his 4–10 record attests, but he did run up 36 saves.

The Cubs liked the swing of first baseman/outfielder Rafael Palmeiro; brought up in midseason, the youngster batted .276. And despite a 6–14 record, the club also was impressed with the strong right arm of twenty-one-year-old Greg Maddux.

Their dismal finish in 1987 belied some bright early-season moments for the team. After a 10–10 April, a surge of 13 wins in 17 games had them in first place on May 20; after that, however, they began playing uninspired ball and gradually floated to the bottom.

On September 7 a dispirited Gene Michael told a reporter that he did not want to manage the team in 1988, which became in effect a firing by resignation. Frank Lucchesi ran the team for the final twenty-five games.

Rafael Palmeiro, who batted .307 for the Cubs in 1988, then became part of the big swap with the Texas Rangers.

Don Zimmer, who played for the Cubs in 1961–1962 and later came back to manage.

On October 29, 1987, Dallas Green resigned as president and general manager. With two years still remaining on his contract, there was speculation that the outspoken Green had been invited to leave. Two weeks later, Green's replacement, with the title of vice-president of baseball operations, was announced—Jim Frey. The skipper of the 1984 division winners had spent the season in the Cubs' radio booth. And now, in a move that was unusual even in baseball's traditional musical chair maneuvers, he was replacing the man who had hired and fired him.

Frey's choice as manager was an old high-school buddy from Cincinnati and another veteran of the game's highways and side roads—Don Zimmer. The little round man, known variously as "Zim," "Zip," and "Popeye," was one of baseball's more respected minds. Once a prized shortstop in the Brooklyn Dodger organization, his career had been damaged by two serious beanings. After spinning through a twelve-year, five-team playing career (that included the Cubs in 1961–62), he had managed at San Diego, Boston, and Texas. A pure-blooded baseball lifer, Zimmer's proud boast was that every paycheck he had ever drawn in his life had come from the game he loved.

Frey and Zimmer immediately went to work to revive a team that was comatose but whose fans were noisily loyal and enthusiastic (the Cubs in 1987 were the first last-place club to draw over two million). On December 8 the team surprised many people by trading their bullpen ace Lee Smith to the Red Sox for right-handers Calvin Schiraldi and Al Nipper. The rationale for the swap was that Smith was looking for a change of scenery; many observers felt that the Cubs could have exacted a better deal for one of the game's premier relievers.

A few months later, Keith Moreland was traded to San Diego along with shortstop Mike Brumley, for pitchers Goose Gossage and Ray Hayward. It was Chicago's intention to convert reliever Schiraldi to a starter and replace Smith with Gossage; but Gossage, the one-time fearsome king of American League relievers with the Yankees, was now thirty-six years old, and his fastball was no longer the intimidating weapon it had been.

To replace Moreland at third, the Cubs signed Vance Law, who had free-agented himself out of Montreal. The team also had fond hopes for Palmeiro and young first base-

All-Star break and 18–8 at season's end. Another positive addition was catcher Damon Berryhill, gradually taking over the job from Jody Davis, who was traded to Atlanta at the end of the season. While Andre Dawson surely was not a disappointment, he did not come close to repeating his thunderous 1987 season (nor did many other hitters who had

Mark Grace: a line-drive bat.

Catcher Damon Berryhill.

man Mark Grace, whose deft way with a bat soon led the Cubs to trade Leon Durham to Cincinnati.

For the Cubs, the 1988 season was a blend of the old and the new, of delights and disappointments. While there was only a fourth-place finish and the team's won–lost record was a drearily familiar 77–85, there were some superb additions to the squad. Grace, coming up from Chicago's Iowa farm club early in the season, flashed a line-drive bat (only 7 home runs), poking away to a .296 average. Palmeiro batted .307, though there was some dissatisfaction with his comparatively low RBI total of 53. The team also found it had a big winner in Greg Maddux, who was 15–3 at the

The end of a tradition: The lights go on at Wrigley for the first time in an official game. It happened on August 8, 1988.

pounded the lively 1987 baseball). Dawson batted .303, hit 24 homers, and drove in 79 runs.

Disappointment derived primarily from that old familiar source of culpability, the mound. Outside of Maddux, no starter was over .500, with Sutcliffe coming in at 13–14. The conversion of Calvin Schiraldi to starter was less than successful (9–13), Gossage had only 13 saves, and Nipper was sidelined much of the time with elbow miseries.

A little-noticed transaction on March 31, 1988, had brought right-hander Mike Bielecki to Chicago from Pittsburgh. Now

twenty-nine years old, Bielecki had at one time been a top prospect in the Pirate organization but had never been able to negotiate the jump to the top. Splitting his time between Chicago and Iowa in 1988, he was 2–2 for the Cubs. Zimmer, however, felt Mike could be a winner.

In 1988, amid the normal flow of elation and inflation endemic to any baseball team in any season, came the end of a Chicago tradition and, in a way, the erasure of the last significant Wrigley fingerprint on the franchise. After much bickering, negotiating, and compromising between the *Tribune* Company, the Chicago City Council, and Wrigley Field neighborhood groups, permission was granted to install lights at the National League's oldest ballpark.

The agreement stipulated a limit of eight night games in 1988 and no more than eighteen a year in the future. Installation of the $5 million lighting system began on April 7. The green grass and ivy-covered walls of Wrigley Field hosted night baseball for the first time on August 7, with the Cubs meeting the Philadelphia Phillies. After three and a half innings, however, rain interrupted play and finally washed out the game. So the Cubs' official home night-game debut was put off to the following evening. With the Mets now their opponents, the Cubs won the game, 6–4.

On December 5, 1988, the Cubs and Texas Rangers enlivened baseball's winter meetings with a hefty nine-man trade. Going to Texas were Rafael Palmeiro and left-handers Jamie Moyer and Drew Hall, in exchange for left-handers Mitch Williams, Paul Kilgus, and Steve Wilson; infielder Curtis Wilkerson; and two minor leaguers.

The key man in the transaction, as far as the Cubs were concerned, was Williams, a high-spirited, extremely hard-working and hard-throwing reliever. The Cubs were desperately in need of a closer—their bullpen had achieved only 29 saves in 56 chances in 1988, a 51.8 percentage that was the worst in the majors.

There was some criticism of the trade in Chicago, particularly toward the disposal of Palmeiro, a .307 hitter in 1988. Frey took the heat and stood firm.

Frey and Zimmer knew that they had improved their club, though not enough to contend with such strong teams as the Mets, Cardinals, and Expos. They agreed privately in the spring that an 81–81 year would be cause for celebration. They could not have known at that time, of course, the kind of production they would get from some untried sources.

Managers of teams that play to losing re-

Mitch ("Wild Thing") Williams, who gave the Cubs everything they had hoped he would in 1989.

cords in spring training are always quick to dismiss the importance of those records. So when the Cubs finished 9–23 in their exhibition games and their fans back in chilly Chicago sighed philosophically, Zimmer said the expected thing: "These games don't mean anything." The little round man was right.

The Cubs jumped off to a good start in 1989. Beginning on May 23, they held the top spot in the East for twenty-five consecutive days before being dislodged by Montreal on June 16 but then regained it the next night by beating the Expos. It was the latest date they had been in first place since 1984, when they won the division.

Zimmer was dismayed when his opening day outfield of Dawson, Mitch Webster, and Jerome Walton all went on the disabled list within five days of each other in early May. The misfortunes, however, turned out to be salutary, for they opened up a spot for Dwight Smith.

Despite some impressive minor-league stats, the twenty-five-year-old Smith had been unable to make the club in spring training. But now he was needed and left the Cubs' Iowa farm club in the American Association, joining his close friend, roommate, and fellow rookie Walton in the outfield. Also brought up at this time was Lloyd McClendon, who broke in sensationally, hitting .359 in his first twenty-two games, with 6 homers and 17 RBIs. (McClendon was an off-season acquisition from the Reds.)

At the All-Star break, the Cubs were 1½ games behind Montreal and were very much a surprise club. Walton and Smith were hitting steadily, contributing to an attack that already included Sandberg, Dawson, an improved Dunston, and the refined bat of sophomore Mark Grace. The team was getting excellent starting pitching from Maddux and Sutcliffe, but the big surprise was Mike Bielecki, who at the age of thirty was suddenly achieving the success that had always eluded him. And coming out of the bullpen was Mitch Williams, more than justifying Frey's

big off-season trade. Nicknamed "Wild Thing" as much for his singular personality as for his sometimes errant fastball, Williams was blazing his way to 36 saves.

And running this squad in his own unpredictable and entertaining style was Zimmer. In a job noted for its generally conservative and orthodox approach, Zimmer was calling for an unusual number of squeeze plays, flashing hit-and-run signs with the bases loaded, calling for pitchouts on two-and-two counts, changing pitchers in the middle of a count, and so on, with a success ratio that more than balanced out the failures in these "gambles."

Walton, the leadoff man the team had needed, ran up a thirty-game hitting streak that was ended on August 21. The streak was the longest by a Cub in the modern era, breaking Ron Santo's twenty-eight-game run, and fell four short of the rookie record set by San Diego's Benito Santiago in 1987.

On August 7, when they beat first-place Montreal, with whom they had been tied, the Cubs took over the division lead for keeps, defending it against assaults form the Expos, Cardinals, and Mets.

When faced with a personnel gap, Frey always moved quickly and efficiently. He acquired third baseman Luis Salazar and outfielder Marvell Wynne from San Diego in late-season deals, and when regular catcher Damon Berryhill was lost for the season on August 18, rookies Rick Wrona and Joe Girardi filled in admirably.

On September 4 the team won its seventy-seventh game, equaling its 1988 total. As Montreal faded and New York struggled, St. Louis continued to hang tough, but the Cubs fought them off, fought off everyone and everything, not least the haunting specters of past collapses. On September 26 Zimmer brought his team through the tape and clinched the division by beating Montreal, 3–2. Their final mark was 93–69, with a 6-game bulge over the second-place Mets. It was only the Cubs' second winning season since 1972, and each had brought a division title.

Jerome Walton, 1989's National League
Rookie of the Year.

Dwight Smith, one of Chicago's talented
rookies of 1989.

Mike Bielecki, Chicago's surprise 18-game winner in 1989.

Greg Maddux, a 19-game winner in 1989.

The Chicago success was highlighted by many splendid season-long individual performances. Walton (.293) and Smith (.324) had been exhilarating surprises, with Smith's average the highest for a Cub rookie since Hack Miller's .352 in 1922. (Walton was voted National League Rookie of the Year, the first Cub to win the designation since Ken Hubbs in 1962. Smith was second in the voting.) Dunston, a .215 hitter over his first fifty games, finished at .278. Grace followed up his fine freshman year with an even better one, batting .314. Dawson dropped to .252 but hit 21 home runs.

For Ryne Sandberg, now beating a path toward the Hall of Fame, it was another Chicago summer of all-around excellence. Along with his .290 batting average, he cracked 30 home runs, most by a Cub second baseman since Hornsby's 39 in 1929. In addition, he committed just 6 errors all season, none of them after June 20. This impeccable ball-handling enabled him to establish a new major-league record for consecutive errorless games by a second baseman, 90.

The team batting average of .261 gave the Cubs the league lead for the second year in a row, the first time a Cubs team had ever done this.

The pitching staff featured a big three: Maddux (19–12), Bielecki (18–7), and Sutcliffe (16–11), backed by Williams and his 36 saves and some high-caliber relief work by Lester Lancaster and left-hander Paul Assenmacher. The staff's 3.43 ERA was its lowest in seventeen years.

For baseball historians the 1989 National League pennant playoff series triggered nostalgic memories. John McGraw and Christy Mathewson and the Polo Grounds were long gone, and the club now called San Francisco home, but they were still the Giants. Memories of 1908 and a onetime highly charged rivalry were evoked.

This time, however, a different conclusion was written. Where in 1908 the Cubs had snatched the pennant from the Giants, in

Lester Lancaster.

1989, thanks primarily to San Francisco first baseman Will Clark, the Giants prevailed.

In Game 1 at Wrigley Field, Clark, who had already hit 1 home run in the game, unloaded a grand-slammer off of Maddux in the top of the fourth that sent the Giants winging to a 9–5 win. The Cubs came back to take Game 2 by the identical 9–5 score, making early work of onetime Chicago ace Rick Reuschel. Grace was the hitting star for the Cubs, with 4 RBIs.

It's the third inning of Game 5 of the 1989 National League Championship Series, and Ryne Sandberg is being tagged out trying to stretch a double into a triple. San Francisco Giants third baseman Matt Williams is applying the tag.

In San Francisco now, the Giants won Game 3 by a 5–4 score when Lancaster fed a 2-run homer to Robbie Thompson in the last of the seventh. Lancaster had replaced Assenmacher with a one-ball, no-strike count on Thompson but came in thinking there were two balls. After throwing what he thought was ball three, Lancaster grooved what he assumed was the "automatic strike," and Thompson jumped all over what was actually a ball-two count, settling the game.

The Giants won Game 4 by a 6–4 score, and the Cubs were one day away from the beginning of winter.

Game 5 culminated in a dramatic confrontation between Will Clark and Mitch Williams. Starter Mike Bielecki pitched brilliantly for six innings, tending diligently to a 1–0 lead. The Giants tied it in the last of the seventh on a Clark triple and a sacrifice fly by Kevin Mitchell. In the last of the eighth, Bielecki suddenly lost his control, walking three straight men with two out. The batter was Clark, who would set league records in playoff competition with 13 hits, 8 runs, 24 total bases, a 1.200 slugging average, and a .650 batting average. In the series he hit 2 home runs, 3 doubles, and a triple. From this pinnacle of success, he now stood in the batter's box with the potential pennant-clinching runs on base. Zimmer brought in Williams, setting up a classic confrontation—

the superb, hard-throwing left-handed reliever versus the superb, hard-hitting left-handed slugger.

Williams blazed over two strikes, then threw a ball. Three more high-voltage fast-balls were fouled off by the tenacious Clark. The Giant first baseman then drove the next pitch on a blurring line past Williams and into center field, scoring 2 runs for a 3–1 Giant lead.

The Cubs fought back in the top of the ninth, stringing together three successive two-out singles against Steve Bedrosian to retrieve one run, but the Giants' ace reliever then retired Sandberg for the final out of the Chicago Cubs' 1989 season.

It was Sandberg who best summed up the season when he said, immediately after the disappointing playoff series, "There's nothing to be ashamed of. We weren't supposed to

A disconsolate Mike Bielecki sits in a littered Cubs dugout after Chicago lost the final game of the NLCS to San Franciso. Mike had pitched six scoreless innings before the Giants came on for a 3–2 pennant-clinching victory.

Mark Grace.

be here, and we did better than anyone expected."

Chicago Cub fans had every right to be proud of the 1989 edition of their favorites and, indeed, took due notice all summer long, giving the team a new home attendance record of 2,491,942.

And so the longest-running team in the National League, the only one never to miss a summer of work and play since William Hulbert organized his league in 1876, completed their 114th season, if not on the game's highest note of triumph, then surely with great satisfaction.

♦ ♦ ♦

Some people have said that the Cubs have become famous for losing. While it may be true that the path leading away from their last world championship finally assumed a length that began traversing entire generations, it is fairer to say that the team has be-

come famous because it is beloved, that the loyalty and enthusiasm of Cub fans have created a unique aura. Losing teams have been known to be abandoned by their followers until, as has been the case more than once in the era of the portable franchise, they are forced to move elsewhere. Cub fans have kept it all in perspective. They seem to feel that almost as important as watching their team win is watching their team.

When a foreign visitor making her way across the United States a few years ago came to Chicago and asked what historic sights were to be seen, she was taken, among other places, to Wrigley Field. There she sat among the Bleacher Bums and got caught up in the raucous elation of a Cub victory. Finally, with delight, she asked, "How long has this been going on?"

"More than 110 years," she was told.

More than 110 years. Baseball's longest-running show, through thick and thin, with all the highs and lows that baseball can supply. Through lively springs (with a few snow flurries) and hot, languid summers into the crisp autumn sunshine. With winds blowing in or out (Chicago meteorologists of a certain character can tell the direction of the wind from the score out at Wrigley).

Cap Anson, Mordecai Brown, Ed Reulbach, and those doggeral-united triplets Tinker, Evers, and Chance are only visiting ghosts at Wrigley, but others have left real spike marks on the turf and cast real shadows on the ivied walls: Grover Cleveland Alexander, Hippo Vaughn, Hack Wilson, Riggs Stephenson, Rogers Hornsby, Billy Herman, Lon Warneke, Bill Lee, Dizzy Dean, Bill Nicholson, Andy Pafko, Ernie ("Mr. Cub") Banks, Billy Williams, Ron Santo, Ferguson Jenkins, and on, up to such latter-day shareholders in baseball's most durable and continuous cavalcade as Ryne Sandberg, Andre Dawson, Mark Grace, Rick Sutcliffe, Jerome Walton, and all the other "bear cubs fleeter than birds" who will play on and on, as long as the ball is round and the game weaves its spell.

APPENDIX

CHICAGO CUBS LEAGUE LEADERS

HOME RUNS

1910	Schulte	10
1911	Schulte	21
1912	Zimmerman	14
1916	Williams	12
1926	Wilson	21
1927	Wilson	30
1928	Wilson	31
1930	Wilson	56
1943	Nicholson	29
1944	Nicholson	33
1952	Sauer	37
1958	Banks	47
1960	Banks	41
1979	Kingman	48
1987	Dawson	49

TRIPLES

1906	Schulte	13
1913	Saier	21
1939	Herman	18
1961	Altman	12
1964	Santo	13
1984	Sandberg	19

DOUBLES

1912	Zimmerman	41
1927	Stephenson	46
1934	Cuyler	42
1935	Herman	57
1981	Buckner	35
1983	Buckner	38

HITS

1906	Steinfeldt	176
1912	Zimmerman	207
1918	Hollocher	161
1935	Herman	227
1940	Hack	191
1941	Hack	186
1944	Cavarretta	197
1970	Williams	205

RUNS BATTED IN

1906	Steinfeldt	83
1911	Schulte	121
1912	Zimmerman	103
1929	Wilson	159
1930	Wilson	190*
1943	Nicholson	128
1944	Nicholson	122
1952	Sauer	121
1958	Banks	129
1959	Banks	143
1987	Dawson	137

BATTING

1912	Zimmerman	.372
1945	Cavarretta	.355
1972	Williams	.333
1975	Madlock	.354
1976	Madlock	.339
1980	Buckner	.324

*Major-league record.

WINS

1909	Brown	27
1912	Cheney	26
1918	Vaughn	22
1920	Alexander	27
1927	Root	26
1929	Malone	22
1930	Malone	20
1932	Warneke	22
1938	Lee	22
1964	Jackson	24
1971	Jenkins	24
1987	Sutcliffe	18

STRIKEOUTS

1909	Overall	205
1918	Vaughn	148
1919	Vaughn	141
1920	Alexander	173
1929	Malone	166
1939	Passeau	137
1946	Schmitz	135
1955	Jones	198
1956	Jones	176
1969	Jenkins	273

EARNED RUN AVERAGE

1902	Taylor	1.33
1906	Brown	1.04
1907	Pfiester	1.15
1918	Vaughn	1.74
1919	Alexander	1.72
1920	Alexander	1.91
1932	Warneke	2.37
1938	Lee	2.66
1945	Borowy	2.13

INDEX